Mythologia Fennica
TAROT

SUSANNA SALO

Mythologia Fennica
TAROT

Embrace ancient Finnish wisdom

ROCKPOOL

A Rockpool book
PO Box 252
Summer Hill
NSW 2130
Australia

rockpoolpublishing.com
Follow us! **f** 🄾 rockpoolpublishing
Tag your images with #rockpoolpublishing

First published by Salakirjat Publishing in 2018
under ISBN 9789527204276
This edition published in 2024 by Rockpool Publishing

ISBN: 9781922786265

The cards *Tree of Life*, *Folk of the Graveyard*, *Liekkiö* and *Dragon* were illustrated by
Laura Kautovaara
Design and typesetting by Sara Lindberg, Rockpool Publishing
Edited by Heather Millar

Printed and bound in China
10 9 8 7 6 5 4 3 2 1

THE CONTENTS
OF THIS TOME

INTRODUCTION

Finnish folklore

The mythology of Finland is down-to-earth and close to nature, saturated with respect for the land's fascinating and gorgeous woodlands and wilderness. The whole of nature and its elements – fire, water, air and earth – were personified and filled with spirits. Every lake, rapid, stream, spring and pond had its own keeper spirit, and so did hidden treasures, graveyards and many other things.

Forests were filled with hiisis, maahinens, elves and sacred animals and beings. The spirits of the long dead ancestors lived in Manala in the bowels of the earth, and mountains and great rocks were the abodes of trolls. At home, among the people, lived the fortune-bringing domestic snakes, and tonttus toiled away to keep the house wealthy and prosperous. Without them the house would fall on hard, bitter times. Neighbours were kept under watchful eye and were often blamed for the misfortunes that befell the house. An envious neighbour could, for example, use the evil eye to bring harm, disease or death upon their neighbour's cattle, or manufacture a para, which would steal grain and milk from others and bring it back to its creator. A skilled witch could even call wolves and bears upon their enemies' cattle.

A fiery eagle guarded the way to Tuonela and the firefox scurried over the mountains of Lapland and set light to the multicoloured northern lights. A swan swam in the river of

1

Tuonela, which was governed by the gigantic, dreaded pike and at the middle of the world stood the proud world column. Shamans travelled along it on spirit journeys, and it held aloft the domelike celestial sphere, which was forged and adorned with stars by Ilmarinen, the cosmic smith. From the North Star opened the gateway to the upper layers of the world, which were numbered nine, same as the lower ones. The upper layers were the abodes of gods, the lower ones the dead, diseased and dark forces.

Such was the world that eventually gave birth to the *Kalevala*.

Kalevala, the national epic of Finland

Elias Lönnrot (1802–1884), a Finnish linguist and physician, published the *Kalevala* for the first time in 1835, and again in 1849 as an updated edition. The epic poem is based on the Finnish and Karelian folk poems he collected from Karelian poem singers, which he edited into a coherent tale about the heroes, villains, champions and monsters of ancient Finland.

In the *Kalevala*, the world is born when the Ilmatar, the female spirit of the air, descends from her clouds to the ocean and is impregnated by the wind and waves. A diving duck makes its nest on her knee, but the eggs fall down on the waves and shatter when the maid moves her knee, and the universe then forms from these shards.

The main protagonists of the *Kalevala* were the old sage Väinämöinen, benevolent smith Ilmarinen and the young and proud Joukahainen. The antagonist of the tale is Louhi, mistress of the rich and cold village of Pohjola, who was a talented witch and the mother of several beautiful maids, whom the men of the village of Kalevala tried to win for their own. The smith Ilmarinen forges the Sampo for Louhi in exchange for her eldest daughter. The Sampo is a wondrous mill that churned endless amounts of salt, grain and gold for its owner. Soon the folk of Kalevala grow envious, and demand to get their share of the machine's riches. When Louhi denies them, Väinämöinen, Ilmarinen and Joukahainen steal it. After a pursuit and a battle on the waves of the sea, the Sampo is destroyed, but some of its fragments wash up on the shores of Kalevala and bring prosperity with them.

These and many other tales have been passed on from one Finnish generation to the next. Folklore and traditions were forwarded by tales and sung poems, and these are the ancient myths and stories that have been collected into this tarot. This book and these cards are a journey into the Finnish mythology.

In closing

It has been spiritually a most expanding and rewarding experience to put this deck together. Unifying Finnish mythologies wisdom with the classic tarot has been fascinating, and it is a pleasure to convey forward the knowledge of our folk. I hope these cards bring you as much joy as they have to me.

Susanna Salo
Helsinki

HOW TO READ THE CARDS

I believe that the purpose of the cards is to mirror both our inner and outer worlds. When interpreting the cards, it is important to trust your intuition and the mental images evoked. The same card can have many different aspects, depending on the situation, and the interpretations given are directional so do not offer definitive answers.

The ancient knowledge behind the cards' illustrations speaks to all of us individually through our inner epiphanies. Each card has several layers of meaning to interpret. They can be studied on a down-to-earth level, focusing on their message as it is, or they can be approached through their symbolical meanings. Old tales contain old wisdom which may be hidden in the cards' descriptions. I hope that the ancient folklore and mythology give different mental images and interpretations for the questions you are seeking to answer.

The cards' characters often depict different aspects within ourselves that either battle each other or work together. For example, Väinämöinen depicts a wise aspect – inner counsellor, teacher and sage – whereas Ilmarinen symbolises someone who takes concrete action.

When reading, trust in the mental images the cards give you. If memories or thoughts relating to the cards' subjects occur, take them into account. Remember: you are the best interpreter for your life. Only you can know what the cards truly mean for your situation. Trust in yourself and in your own vision, which these cards will make clearer. If a question doesn't seem to open through the cards or you feel uncertain, you can always do another reading or draw more cards for further questions. If I have two options to choose from, I often draw cards for both.

The spreads

I recommend using traditional spreads and always interpreting all the cards of the spread as a whole. The cards may also bring to your mind meanings that differ from those given here, so stay open to them.

Card of the day

Shuffle the cards and spread them in a circle or semicircle, facedown. Close your eyes and pick 1 to 3 cards. Then turn them, one by one, and let your consciousness rest in them. Let your mind open itself to each card's message and energy. If you wish, read the description in this guidebook. Continue to ponder the card's message and your relationship to it during the day. I like to draw a card at the start of the working day. That way the card will be in my mind all day and I may receive new aspects and content.

Review

This is a good way to clarify your situation. Shuffle the cards while focusing on your question. You may also seek general advice from the cards: simply keep your mind open while shuffling.

Lay the cards facedown in a shape, then draw 3.

- Card 1 depicts your past or its influence in your situation.
- Card 2 is the present and your current situation; the key to your question.
- Card 3 symbolises the future or the solution.

Draw additional cards if necessary.

Sound advice

Quieten your mind and focus on your question. Draw 5 cards and lay them out facedown as shown. One by one, turn the cards over from 1 to 5 and open yourself to each card's message.

- Card 1 depicts the problem or question at hand.
- Card 2 represents your goal; where you're headed.
- Card 3 symbolises the things that you should forfeit or which you are ready to relinquish.
- Card 4 tells the things you are receptive to; what you're missing in your life.
- Card 5 represents the sound advice; the answer to your question.

THE
MAJOR
ARCANA

– 0 –

THE BEGINNING
The Fool

THE BEGINNING

THE FOOL

*Keywords: courage to take risks, infinite possibilities,
forming new ideas, listen to your heart.*

In the *Kalevala*, the world originated from the egg of a diving
duck. Ilmatar, the female spirit of the air, descended from the
sky to the primordial sea, Sarajas, transforming into the female

spirit of the water. She swam through the endless waves when a diving duck, searching for a place to nest, flew past and spied the spirit's knee emerging from the sea. The bird built its nest on the knee and laid six golden and one iron egg, which began to hatch. Ilmatar moved her knee as it began to warm up, and the eggs rolled into the water and shattered. The different layers and fundamental things of the world formed from one egg, and that is why the newborn world was a coherent entirety.

MESSAGE: The primordial sea Sarajas corresponds to the elemental chaos or the state of nothingness that preceded the world's creation. Though according to folklore, the void wasn't utterly empty, for the female spirits of air and water inhabited it. First there was only air, from whence water diverged. The egg symbolises the seed of new life. This card indicates a new beginning for you – something is about to be born, and the state of chaos and emptiness that precedes it is gaining its new, organised form. Have faith in the creative forces of the universe and boldly take a leap of faith into the unknown. A sincere attitude towards life and its ever-renewing wonders opens up new possibilities. This card encourages you to gallantly begin new endeavours and trust in your own infinite possibilities to form your life exactly the way you want to it be. Seize the new opportunities coming your way, and give in to the flow of life.

ILMARINEN
The Magician

ILMARINEN

THE MAGICIAN

Keywords: brilliant intelligence, intuitive action, creation, ideas and visions gaining concrete form.

Ilmarinen was an old god of air and wind who controlled the weather and storm winds, born when he fanned the flames of his forge. He was also the protector of travellers. When the cosmos was created, Ilmarinen forged the celestial sphere and adorned it with stars. A mighty blacksmith, he forged wondrous things from practically nothing. For Louhi, the Mistress of Pohjola, he made the Sampo in exchange for the hand of her beautiful daughter, the Maid of Pohjola. When Ilmarinen began to forge the wondrous Sampo, he didn't have tools, a forge or a smithy. Furthermore, Louhi had ordered what materials Ilmarinen could use, and they were unsuitable. Nevertheless, Ilmarinen began his work, as impossible as it seemed, for he had something that is required from a true magician – he was able to forge concrete wonders founded on his own visions.

MESSAGE: The smith symbolises the forging of strong, new forms in your life. Ilmarinen forged a golden plough and an eagle, which helped him overcome Louhi's tasks. This reflects the forging of your higher self as you overcome doubt and fear. Gold symbolises the divine light, love and the great treasures within you. The eagle represents immense strength and boundless freedom, which you must use wisely. Don't give up once you discover your gifts, even if you don't at first succeed. Work on your ideas and you will begin to soar when the time is right. Do everything you can to make your dreams come true. Trust your vision, instincts and strength – dare to show others what you are made of.

– II –

**MOTHER OF
LEMMINKÄINEN**
The High Priestess

MOTHER OF LEMMINKÄINEN

THE HIGH PRIESTESS

*Keywords: intuition, healer, inner
strength, self-confidence.*

When Lemminkäinen proposed to the Maid of Pohjola, her
mother, Louhi, gave him three difficult tasks. He succeeded in
two, but on the third, he was supposed to shoot a swan, but an

enemy killed him and he fell into the black river and was carried to Tuonela, where the dead linger. There, his corpse was hacked to pieces. Before he left, Lemminkäinen declared to his mother that a brush stuck in the wall would begin to bleed should he die. To her horror, the mother saw blood dripping from the brush. She looked for her son far and wide, turning to the moon and the sun who confirmed her son was dead. The smith Ilmarinen made her a rake and she searched the river, finding her son's mutilated corpse. Setting the pieces on the riverbank, she joined them until Lemminkäinen's body was again intact, but lifeless. The mother called to a bee, which flew through nine layers of heaven to fetch the liquid of life from above. Mother anointed her son with the balm, and Lemminkäinen was resurrected.

MESSAGE: The love of the mother was able to conquer death through powerful intuition and strong will. She conversed with the moon and sun, representing the subconscious and the conscious, leading to a wise, comprehensive understanding of her situation. The bee symbolises love, industry and willingness to help. Her son's return from the dead represents the understanding of life, death and rebirth – the comprehensive awakening within on the soul level. The mutilation of his body represents the last stage of a shamanic initiation, where the shaman dies to his old life and is reborn as a sage. The veils separating the levels of consciousness are lifted and an understanding of your life more extensively on a deeper level becomes available.

LOUHI
The Empress

LOUHI

THE EMPRESS

Keywords: protection of inner and outer wellbeing, feminine wisdom, decisiveness, integrity.

Louhi was the Mistress of Pohjola, the birthplace of all diseases and ailments plaguing mankind. She was also responsible for gales, cold winds and dangerous woodland creatures, except the bear. Her three sons, Rujo, Rampa and Perisokea (Ugly, Lame and Blind), would cast upon people the torments birthed by their mother. Louhi also had daughters famous for their beauty, who the heroes of Kalevala tried to win. The central mountain of the world, Pohjola's great Stone-hill, was the place where Louhi locked up the moon and the sun and the Sampo, and it was also the place where diseases were banished when someone was cured using a spell. Louhi commanded the great armed forces of Pohjola and led them herself during the raid of Sampo and the pursuit of Lemminkäinen after he had killed the Master of Pohjola. Louhi gave impossible tasks to her daughters' suitors and demanded great compensations, such as the wondrous Sampo.

MESSAGE: Louhi may be seen as an evil entity, but there is also admirable grandness in her, combined with intuitive sensitivity and wisdom, the properties of a strong female leader. These qualities are necessary for those wishing to control their own lives. Louhi doesn't bend to unnecessary compromise – she is wise not to give her treasures or power up easily when aspiring to secure the wellbeing of her kingdom. This card refers to a person with a strong will and good self-esteem. Despite her strength Louhi is caring – she doesn't need advice from others regarding her affairs. Use your wisdom and deep understanding when making decisions. Even when acting independently, don't forget the needs of others. As Louhi in the end allowed her daughter to decide for herself who to marry, allow those near you to decide what's best for them.

THE MAJOR ARCANA

VÄINÄMÖINEN
The Emperor

VÄINÄMÖINEN

THE EMPEROR

*Keywords: sage, will to act, control over
one's own life, responsibility.*

One of the most important characters in Finnish mythology,
Väinämöinen was a sage and healer from the moment of
his birth, and so ancient he was almost as old as the world.

The essential elements of the world already existed when he was born, but he had an active role in the creation of human culture. His inner strength and iron will helped him succeed in almost anything he set his mind to. Originally Väinämöinen was a god of water – the word *väinä* means a wide, calmly streaming river – and in stories he often travels by boat. Steady and strong-willed, he was adamant in his decisions, and his level-headedness, calmness and wisdom made him an excellent leader. He often advised Ilmarinen and Lemminkäinen. Striving to do his best when faced with challenges, he took control in difficult situations. His enchanting skill with the kantele made the whole of creation, even the sun and the moon, listen to him play. The keeper of traditions and poem-singing who always wanted to find the truth in all things, Väinämöinen wouldn't accept something being left half-done. Despite being a mighty sage he didn't boast, nor was he proud.

MESSAGE: This card corresponds to the Emperor of the classical tarot deck. You have strength and wisdom that can help you overcome any obstacle. The card refers to highly perceptive and functional judgement, and to the good qualities of a leader. True leadership doesn't come from domination, but from supporting others in utilising their strengths. Authority and the control of situations is always followed by great responsibility. Aim to act wisely, with consideration and by trusting in your life experience. Remain calm and find out everything about the things affecting your situation. Make independent decisions, and don't submit to the whims of others.

THE SHAMAN
The Hierophant

THE SHAMAN

THE HIEROPHANT

Keywords: truth, spiritual master,
true knowledge, inner guide.

The shaman was the spiritual leader of hunter–gatherer communities. Acting as an intermediary between the living and the world of spirits, the shaman travelled between the world's layers in search of remedies for people's ailments. Often a solitary figure, the shaman often lived on the outskirts of their community, as if near the border of two worlds. The shaman had to go through a long, often painful initiation lasting seven years learning to comprehend the different levels of the world, searching for knowledge and making connections to helpers. The last stage of the initiation was the shaman's death and dismemberment. This happened on a spiritual, not physical, level. The symbolic death represented the ending of the initiate's former life and the beginning of a new role as shaman. The initiation itself was about dismantling, comprehending and rebuilding one's own psyche. True healers always begin their journey by healing themselves.

MESSAGE: It is wise to regard with suspicion spiritual teachers who spew their wisdom without practising it in their own life. The world is full of such guides and counsellors, but there's no greater hierophant for you than yourself. Only you can know what feels real to you and what doesn't. You won't become a shaman overnight, but life's purpose for you is to find your own strengths and weaknesses. You may notice how the storms, joys, challenges and sorrows of life have honed and taught you and made you who you are. Everyone is the shaman of their own life, practising the calling of their own soul. This card symbolises becoming a master in your own life. If you don't feel like a master yet, it means you're still on your way. The journey never ends.

THE WEDDING OF POHJOLA
The Lovers

THE WEDDING OF POHJOLA

THE LOVERS

Keywords: attraction, romance, commitment,
awareness through a relationship.

Ilmarinen succeeded in Louhi's tasks and was to marry the Maid
of Pohjola. He had ploughed the field of adders, bridled the
bear of Manala and caught the gigantic pike of Tuonela. He had

also forged the Sampo as payment for his bride. The Maid, who had begun to fancy the crafty smith, aided him in his efforts. The great Wedding of Pohjola was held in the lovers' honour. All of Kalevala and Pohjola, even the wretched, poor, lame, crippled and disfigured, were invited to the magnificent feast. Only Lemminkäinen was left uninvited by Louhi's command, for he was a quarrelsome man and there was to be no strife at the wedding. After the feast it was time for the bride's sorrowful parting songs as she left her beloved home and dear mother. She was told to wipe her tears and prepare for her new life. Before the bride and groom left on their sleigh, they were advised to honour one another and work hard for mutual happiness.

MESSAGE: Ilmarinen and the Maid's love was harmonious, balanced and devoted. This card symbolises attraction and opposites striving to unite. It is about becoming aware through love and relationship, but also about unifying opposite energies within yourself. It also reminds you that no relationship is without its hardships. The purpose of the relationship is to become free through it. This happens by letting go of expectations and accepting your significant other's uniqueness and individuality. Accepting them just as they are is the path to find your own wholeness. Louhi's tasks were meant to hone and test potential suitors; the spiritual growth attained through facing the challenges helped the men find talents and strengths hidden within them. The prize was the Maid of Pohjola, who has been compared to the higher self.

**LAMENTATION
OF THE BOAT**
The Chariot

LAMENTATION OF THE BOAT

THE CHARIOT

*Keywords: journey of life, preparation,
finding and following your own path.*

Ever since Ilmarinen had made the Sampo for Louhi, life had
begun to turn sourer in Kalevala. He and Väinämöinen planned
a voyage to Pohjola to retrieve the Sampo, which produced

fortune and riches. Väinämöinen heard lamentation coming from behind a patch of tall grass on the shore. He came upon a crying boat, mourning the fact it wasn't seaworthy. Väinämöinen took pity on the boat and repaired it. He launched it on the waves, then as they set sail, Lemminkäinen called out to them from a headland, and they took him aboard also. The heroes faced many dangers on the way. The boat ran aground on the back of a giant pike that Väinämöinen then killed, and from whose jaw he made the first kantele, while Lemminkäinen succeeded in a difficult rafting, although he couldn't wrest the Sampo free from Stone-hill of Pohjola or catch the giant pike. It was only when Väinämöinen put the folk of Pohjola into a slumber that they woke to see the Sampo gone.

MESSAGE: The boat represents the body, the vehicle the soul uses to travel through life. The rotting boat laments its fate until Väinämöinen, Ilmarinen and Lemminkäinen, representing the different sides of consciousness, hop onboard and head for adventure. This card symbolises the passing of time, but the boat is nevertheless meant to sail the waters of life towards new adventures. Nothing is lost even if the previous voyages have passed and your boat is lying on the shore pining about its fate. Set your course towards a new journey as Väinämöinen did, to find new aspects in himself. No one can live your life for you; the keys to your happiness are in your own hands. Have courage – try something new and trust life. Cast yourself into the stream.

LEMMINKÄINEN
Strength

LEMMINKÄINEN

STRENGTH

*Keywords: courage, powerful drive,
adventurous spirit, restlessness.*

Lemminkäinen was the fairest and most daring of Kalevala's heroes, an ardent soul filled with unquenchable wanderlust. His name refers to both fire and love, and he is said to be the son of fire. Lemminkäinen was a bold, handsome warrior who beamed magnetic energy all around him. His social skills allowed him to charm everyone, and he was often the centre of attention. No one in Kalevala had as many relationships as Lemminkäinen. He married Kyllikki, who hailed from a good family, but couldn't stay still for long because of his restless mind. Lemminkäinen didn't find peace at home at his fiancée's side, for in his soul burned a fiery passion for new adventures in far-away lands. Kyllikki and Lemminkäinen made their vows which both of them later broke. The only true love in Lemminkäinen's life was his mother, who was prepared to do anything for her son.

MESSAGE: This card refers to courage, strength, skill and following your own nature. Lemminkäinen's ardent soul was honed in the passage of time by his innumerable escapades and incidents. Symbolising youth, passion for life, lust for adventure and curiosity, Lemminkäinen's tale is one of growth: he tries and attempts until he learns. Always rushing into action without thinking or caring about the consequences, he landed himself in serious trouble more than once. Lemminkäinen is also a perfect example of a person who hasn't resolved his relationship with his parents. He may be somewhat narcissistic because of his strong mother who worshipped him from the moment of his birth. That is why the card suggests pondering your relationship with your own parents, and to grow independent and strong. Believe in yourself and don't be afraid of life's adventures: far-off lands and social circles are waiting to be conquered.

ANTERO VIPUNEN
The Hermit

ANTERO VIPUNEN

THE HERMIT

Keywords: solitude, finding inner guidance, turning within.

When Väinämöinen proposed to the Maid of Pohjola she gave him a task: to fashion a boat by using his knowledge and spells. Väinämöinen began his work, but three words were missing from his spell, and the boat was left incomplete. He went to seek out Antero Vipunen, a gigantic sage who had lain dead for so long that trees were growing on him. When Väinämöinen woke the sleeping sage by jamming a spear into his mouth, the old giant was displeased and refused Väinämöinen's requests. He yawned so widely that Väinämöinen slipped, fell into his mouth and was swallowed. When Vipunen refused to let him out, Väinämöinen didn't panic; he accepted the situation and began to think how to outsmart the ancient sage. He built a forge inside Vipunen's stomach and the sage began to feel smoke rising up his throat. Väinämöinen reminded him that although sages went to their graves, there was no reason their knowledge had to go with them. Finally Vipunen yielded and began to sing his words of power, including the words Väinämöinen needed and the grateful Väinämöinen climbed out.

Message: When Väinämöinen went after the sage's knowledge and fell into his mouth, he achieved an altered state of consciousness, as the shaman does to travel through the different layers of the world. This is how Väinämöinen could get his hands on hidden knowledge. Vipunen was a hermit who valued his peace and possessed knowledge which many a seeker wanted. This card urges you to seek the truth and your own inner light. You can find the wise guide within by becoming quiet. Being alone doesn't have to mean the same as being lonely — it can be a fruitful, positive experience regarding your own spiritual development. Seek out the fountain of wisdom within you.

SAMPO
Wheel of Fortune

SAMPO

WHEEL OF FORTUNE

*Keywords: wealth, fortune, a great
breakthrough, creativity.*

As a reward for forging the Sampo, a magical mill producing
endless wealth, Louhi promised Ilmarinen the Maid of Pohjola
as a bride. Louhi buried the Sampo in Pohjola's great Stone-hill,

guarding it night and day. Pohjola began to gain wealth, but misery reigned supreme in Kalevala. When the Maid of Pohjola died, the men of Kalevala headed to Pohjola. Louhi wouldn't share the Sampo, so Väinämöinen lulled the people to sleep using his kantele. The men broke into the Stone-hill and carried the Sampo to their boat. On the way home Lemminkäinen couldn't control his joy and began to sing, waking the folk of Pohjola. When Louhi saw the Sampo was gone, she set sail in a great warship. When they hit a rock and the ship sank, Louhi turned herself into an eagle, took her forces on her back and flew to their enemies. As they battled, the Sampo slipped from Louhi's claws, shattering. The waves carried some pieces to Kalevala, bringing fortune and prosperity with them.

MESSAGE: Ilmarinen brought the Sampo to life using his vision and skills to create something never seen before. Sampo represents an idea that brings wealth; using your vision and skills, you can create a Sampo of your own. However, all good ideas should be shared. The moral behind the story of Sampo is that no one can hoard all the fortune alone. Louhi didn't want to share the Sampo although it would have churned enough wealth for all, and the raiders fared no better. Sampo slipped through their fingers, because universal riches belong to everyone. Sampo fell into the sea, enriching the water, the element of emotions. Fortune is an outcome of your own spiritual growth. Sharing your inner wealth with others will multiply it. Use your imagination creatively and wisely.

– XI –

LOVE RIVALS
Justice

LOVE RIVALS

JUSTICE

Keywords: choice, honesty, negotiation
skill, resolving differences.

Louhi was eager to join Väinämöinen's mighty family with her own through marriage. She promised him her daughter if he forged the Sampo for her. When he wasn't able, he promised to send his brother Ilmarinen. On his way home Väinämöinen saw the Maid and proposed to her, and she demanded he carve a boat using only his spells. Back home Väinämöinen tried to persuade his brother to forge the Sampo for Louhi, but Ilmarinen wasn't willing. Väinämöinen tricked him and sang a wind that carried the smith away. Once in Pohjola, Ilmarinen also became infatuated with the Maid, and agreed to forge the Sampo in exchange for the young lady. Meanwhile Väinämöinen visited Antero Vipunen, got the missing words, finished his boat and set sail to Pohjola. Annikki, Ilmarinen's sister, asked him where he was going. Väinämöinen admitted his intent, and Annikki warned Ilmarinen other men were after his bride. Ilmarinen quickly spurred his horse back towards Pohjola. Louhi saw the two suitors coming and advised her daughter to take Väinämöinen, but the Maid had grown to like Ilmarinen. Louhi gave Ilmarinen three additional tasks, which he successfully completed with the Maid's help. In the end Louhi gave in – the young couple were engaged.

MESSAGE: The Maid of Pohjola's situation wasn't an easy one, for if she listened to her heart she would be going against her mother's will. But if she had chosen Väinämöinen against her own feelings, she would have suffered greatly. In any case she had to let one of her suitors down. This card symbolises demands and expectations coming from several directions. Trust your own inner judgement about what supports your own spiritual growth in the best possible way. Others will come to accept and adapt to your decision in time.

DUELLING SINGERS
The Hanged Man

DUELLING SINGERS

THE HANGED MAN

Keywords: stagnation, competition, new perspectives, change of course.

News of Väinämöinen's skill with song reached the ears of young Joukahainen who grew jealous. He decided to challenge the old man to a song-duel. Väinämöinen wasn't eager to fight and asked what Joukahainen thought he knew better than anyone else. Joukahainen began to recite all he knew about deep subjects, and even claimed to have had some hand in creating the world. Irritated, Väinämöinen boomed that he had been present when the world was created, and he didn't recall seeing the young upstart there. When Joukahainen saw he couldn't beat the old man with his knowledge, he challenged him to a sword fight. Väinämöinen had had enough of the young man's insolence, and he began to sing so the lakes spilled over and the ground trembled. He sang for Joukahainen to be sunk into a bog up to his armpits. Joukahainen begged for mercy and promising Väinämöinen anything if he would let him go: his boat, his horse, his sister Aino. This piqued the old sage's interest and he lifted Joukahainen back on solid ground.

MESSAGE: Joukahainen's pride prevented him from backing down when it would've been wise. He was at an impasse, and there seemed to be no escape until he offered his sister – but Aino wasn't his to give. He burdened her with the consequences of his own stupidity, and the innocent girl later drowned herself to escape her fate, thus dying in her brother's stead. Song-duels were about humility and respecting one another, and by holding on to pride, both Joukahainen and Väinämöinen lost something irreplaceable. Breaking free from narrow perspectives may be painful but spiritual growth is a part of life. Competing and comparing aren't usually fruitful ways to interact with others. As the old Finnish proverb goes: 'Jealousy takes fish from water, hate barrens the fields.'

LASS OF TUONELA
Death

LASS OF TUONELA

DEATH

Keywords: transition to a new stage of life, old giving way to new, freedom from old shackles, rebirth.

When Väinämöinen came to Tuonela on his search for the words of power, he called to the Lass of Tuonela, whose purpose was to ferry the dead souls over the black river, to ferry him across. But

THE MAJOR ARCANA

the girl wouldn't take anyone living on her boat, so Väinämöinen tried to deceive her, to no avail. Finally Väinämöinen confessed he was after the missing words. The Lass agreed to take the sage over the river, but warned him he would not get the words and would not return. In Tuonela, Väinämöinen was given an uncomfortable bed of snakes to rest upon while the dead wove nets across the river to prevent him from escaping. Sensing doom, Väinämöinen couldn't sleep, so he transformed himself into a snake and slithered between the nets.

The swan that swam in the river of Tuonela, which Lemminkäinen was unsuccessful in trying to shoot when Louhi gave him the task, was a soul-bird that couldn't be killed. The soul-bird refers to an old belief that a person's soul transforms into a bird upon death and leaves the body with the last breath. We carry on as the soul-bird, although our worldly journey comes to an end.

MESSAGE: This card doesn't point to an actual death but to changes on a physical level, to letting go of old things and, most importantly, to a new beginning. There are moments in life when you are meant to turn over a new leaf, to let everything that has become obsolete die away. This releases you from old ties and renews life in an essential way. The process becomes painful only when opposed. By accepting change and the fact that life itself is change, you can become free from the torments and fears caused by it. Dare to let go of that which is leaving and be open to that which is coming in its place.

XIV

MAID OF POHJOLA
Temperance

MAID OF POHJOLA

TEMPERANCE

Keywords: talents and gifts, inner change, significant step.

The Maid of Pohjola sat on a rainbow weaving a golden cloth. Väinämöinen stopped his horse when he passed by and saw her. He tried to entice her to go to Kalevala with him to be his bride. The Maid didn't know what to do, so she challenged her suitor to demonstrate his skills by cutting a horsehair in half, knotting an egg and peeling a stone. To the Maid's chagrin Väinämöinen succeeded easily, so she challenged him to an impossible task – to carve a boat without the use of his hands only using spells and songs. Väinämöinen began his work but found out he was missing three words from his spells to finish the boat. To find them, he made the dangerous trip to Tuonela, from where he had to escape. Then he sought out Antero Vipunen, the ancient sage, and succeeded in pressuring the words out of him. Väinämöinen finished the boat and set sail to Pohjola to collect the Maid, but meanwhile smith Ilmarinen had also made claims for the girl by forging the Sampo for her mother, Louhi.

MESSAGE: This card represents learning new things and using what you already know to succeed in difficult tasks and situations. The prize you're after may not fall into your lap after you've mastered new skills, but the skills themselves are the prize. Things don't always go as you would've liked, but in the end you realise you have learned something you wouldn't have otherwise, had things gone the way you intended. The Maid of Pohjola urges you to bring creative forces together with the energies of the earth. Use your abilities wisely and take challenging tasks on without fear. Remember that failure is also an important part of life, and there's no reason to be afraid of it.

XV

THE DEVIL
The Devil

THE DEVIL

THE DEVIL

Keywords: sexuality, liberation from old moral attitudes, individuality, freedom of choice.

In the Finnish folktales the Devil was close to humans and often willing to help those in need, while God resided far away in heaven. The Devil enjoyed spending time around gamblers and drunks, trying to lead them to their doom. All sorts of frivolity and excess lured the Devil, but he also helped those who were in trouble and punished those who sinned. The Devil would bargain over people's immortal souls and could appear at a weak moment offering money or success to a desperate person in exchange for their soul. A pact with the Devil meant an easy idle life, but in the end the Devil would always come to collect what was his. If blackbirds gathered in the trees around the house when someone was dying, it was held as a sign of this pact. It was said the birds came to take the soul with them.

Message: Despite its reputation, the Devil is not an ill card; it may represent the will to live free from moral codes. The Devil's energy is powerfully renewing and creative, so this card may also mean questioning moral standards and rebellion against authority. It tells of a need to do what feels good for yourself instead of obeying the instructions of others. It can also be a sign of tensions in a relationship where one party is submissive to the other. If you use your willpower correctly, you will notice that you always have the freedom to choose from multiple possibilities. Be careful not to moralise around what others do; focus on your own energies and how you want to live your life. This may lead to conflict, but it's still the only way to freedom. Dare to live life to its fullest and to be who you truly are.

XVI

THE GREAT OAK
The Tower

THE GREAT OAK

THE TOWER

*Keywords: purification, new clarity, fundamental
inner change, healing, collapse of old structures.*

Väinämöinen rose from the primordial sea onto a barren earth,
and at his behest Sampsa Pellervoinen, the spirit of vegetation
and fertility, sowed the lands and bogs full of trees and plants.

One sapling didn't just sprout – the acorn rooted and turned into a beautiful sapling. The oak grew swiftly and soon its crown covered the sky. Clouds were snared in its branches and life become dark and unbearable for the great oak prevented the sun and moon from shining. Väinämöinen turned to the folk of water for help, and a small, black man ascended from the waves. He looked so tiny and insignificant Väinämöinen didn't believe he could help fell the oak. But the man began to change, growing as tall as the tree. He struck the great oak and with three strikes the mighty tree came crashing down.

Message: When the great oak was gone, the moon and the sun were free to shine once more. The sun and moon symbolise the light of consciousness and the subconscious. The snared clouds represent thoughts that are shackled instead of being allowed to roam freely and creatively. This card may symbolise some outer circumstances that make the life force fade. The one who comes to the rescue is the small man from the sea. The sea represents the area of the subconscious and unconscious, whereas the man portrays determination and inner strength that grows as strong as the present situation requires, to help you to sort out your problems. The oak was not in balance with the rest of the world, and its felling was imperative. Life has its own ways to set free the things that have become stagnant or run their course, as well as guide relationships towards new growth.

XVII

THE NORTH STAR
The Star

THE NORTH STAR

THE STAR

Keywords: opening up to the higher levels of consciousness, creative visions, fountain of wisdom.

According to the old Finnish belief, the celestial sphere was like a gigantic tent held aloft by the magnificent world pillar. In the middle of the sky was the North Star which didn't move.

It seemed to be the centre of the universe, with other stars and constellations circling around it. The stars were the people's compass, a way to tell time during the night, predict the weather and the impending lunar and solar eclipses. The North Star was the most reliable way to tell where the north was. The North Star was also imagined to be a gateway to the upper layers of heaven and the abode of gods. The concept of a universe that consists of layers is an ancient one. The layers were separated by celestial spheres with an opening in the middle that led to other layers. These gateways were also used by shamans who travelled to other layers on their spirit journeys.

MESSAGE: This card symbolises light, guidance and inner vision. The North Star is a sign of your ability to elevate your thought process to higher levels of understanding and to other dimensions. Ideas and inspiration come to you at the speed of light as intuitive hunches and in dreams. It is wise to follow these visions if you wish to find your purpose in life. If you have already found it, this card's purpose is to help you stay the course. The layers of heaven represent the higher states of consciousness, attainable through meditation, trance or dreaming. It was also thought the path to the afterlife began from the North Star and the souls of the dead rose up to the star to begin their journey. To follow your own star is to fulfil your own soul path or purpose in life.

XVIII

GATES OF POHJOLA
The Moon

GATES OF POHJOLA

THE MOON

Keywords: challenges, wrong choices, freedom from delusions, gateway to new levels of consciousness.

The moon controlled the rhythm of life and the activities of everyday life were synchronised to its phases. The lunar eclipse was believed to be caused by Rahko, a mythical thief who climbed to the moon and painted it black with tar so its light wouldn't reveal his larcenous deeds. The night was traditionally the time of beasts, ghosts and thieves, which the moon illuminated. The road that led to the cold village of Pohjola was filled with obstacles and challenges. The traveller was forced to walk on the points of needles and blades of swords, past mythological beasts such as a fiery eagle or giant snake. The Stone-hill of Pohjola was heavily fortified, and the only way in was through the Gates of Pohjola. There were nine locks and nine gates framed by snakes and guarded by a dog.

MESSAGE: The moon's energy is feminine, changing and obscure. It symbolises our subconscious instincts and the world of dreams, and this card represents the journey to the worlds below to the dwellings of your subconscious. Your fears, instincts and repressed memories that rear their ugly heads in the form of beasts live there, but so do your unconscious hopes and yet to be discovered talents as well. The way to Pohjola is filled with dangers and challenges and it represents the act of purification from vain, pride and delusion that prevents your true self from coming forth. It is an initiation rite that many native peoples have practised at difficult phases of life. The way leading to the Gates symbolises a journey from which there is no return, the path of the shaman. It won't be easy, so you must stay strong and true to yourself. Boldly face the things you've tried to hide from yourself.

XIX

THE MAJOR ARCANA

LIBERATION OF THE SUN
The Sun

LIBERATION OF THE SUN

THE SUN

*Keywords: provider of fertility and warmth,
creative power, harmonic relationships,
powerful light of consciousness.*

The whole of creation halted to listen when Väinämöinen first played his kantele, even the heavenly lights, and that's when

Louhi grabbed the sun and the moon and hid them in the Stone-hill of Pohjola. A seemingly eternal night fell upon Kalevala. Väinämöinen found out where the lights were hidden but was unable to open the locks. The disappointed sage returned home and asked Ilmarinen to forge keys, a three-headed rake and spears with which to wrestle the sun and the moon free. Louhi transformed into a bird and flew to Kalevala to see what the smith was up to. Ilmarinen noticed the grey raptor at his window and the bird began to speak, praising Ilmarinen's skill and inquiring what the smith was making. Ilmarinen replied that he was fashioning a neck-shackle with which Louhi would be bound to a boulder, and the frightened Louhi flew back to Pohjola and set the sun and moon free once more.

MESSAGE: The Stone-hill of Pohjola, the world mountain, symbolises perspective and clarity which, when opened, releases the energy of the sun back into your life. The sun symbolises strength, energy, clarity and knowledge. Louhi ascended to a higher spiritual level and realised she had to set the sun and moon free herself. The key therefore is in elevating your consciousness to a high enough state that you can understand how locks are shackling energy within you, and to learn to be free from the restraints and obstacles you have created for yourself. Great light and energy are returning to your life after a long, dark period. Spring is coming, a time of renewal and powerful growth; blossoming is at hand and a new kind of energy fills you. Limitless amounts of strength are hiding within, and now you can express yourself perfectly and creatively.

XX

FEAST OF POHJOLA
Judgement

FEAST OF POHJOLA

JUDGEMENT

*Keywords: perceptive and discerning mind, open
to criticism, learning through new experiences.*

A great wedding feast had been arranged for smith Ilmarinen
and the Maid of Pohjola. Everyone was invited except for well-
known troublemaker Lemminkäinen, who decided to attend

anyway. After he sat on the Master's seat and demanded ale and food, the Master of Pohjola challenged him to a sword fight. Lemminkäinen struck the Master's head off and impaled it on a spear. Louhi rallied her troops, but Lemminkäinen changed into an eagle and fled home, where his mother advised him to flee to an island beyond nine seas. Lemminkäinen sailed to the island where his father had also once lain low. During the time he was there, he charmed all the wives and widows of the island, and the island's men prepared to murder him. Lemminkäinen was forced to flee once again. Back home he was greeted by ruin and destruction, for the soldiers of Pohjola had destroyed everything looking for him. Lemminkäinen found his mother hiding in the forest and promised her he would rebuild the house. However, secretly, he was planning a raid to Pohjola as vengeance for the destruction.

MESSAGE: Lemminkäinen's fiery soul drove him from one trouble to another, and many an innocent suffered for this. His mother protected her son with her life and suffered the consequences, and by doing so unwittingly encouraged her son to always undertake one raid after another. This card calls for good judgement and taste, which Lemminkäinen didn't possess. But good judgement doesn't mean criticising others. When you cease to criticise, your own understanding grows. Try to see people and situations without prejudices, and accept things as they are. This card urges you to abandon your old, narrow perspective and to see things from a broader one. Act according to your own calling. Try to steer your life in a constructive direction.

XXI

THE TREE OF LIFE
The World

THE TREE OF LIFE

THE WORLD

Keywords: universe, to become complete, travelling.

In Finnish folklore, the sacred world tree is a birch or an oak, sometimes depicted as being on fire with a fiery eagle on top. The tree of life was said to grow on an island surrounded by a river or the primordial sea. The tree grew on top of a world mountain at the centre of a well seen as the source of life, its roots burrowing nine fathoms deep. The tree's crown reached to the heavens and on top was a golden cradle, used to lower souls born on the tree's branches down to earth. Around the cradle was a gathering place of souls, and the gateway to the worlds of gods. At the centre of Siberian and Finno-Ugric worlds was a world pillar, like a branchless world tree, holding aloft the heavens – the backbone of the cosmos. The world was held in place by a golden column, and in the middle of the sky was the North Star, with a wheel on top of which the celestial sphere turned. Associated to the tree of life are life-giving and protecting goddesses – three fates who watched over the spring and controlled the sacred powers of the world's hub.

MESSAGE: The tree is a metaphor for individual growth and development through life. Deep roots symbolise your connection to the spiritual wellspring. High-reaching branches represent your ability to express yourself. Countless tree leaves symbolise the things you may create through your talents. You've become a pillar that connects down-to-earth practical knowledge to cosmic visions and high ideals. You know how to make use of these seemingly opposing forces in your life, and you may reach for even greater accomplishments and ideas. Experiences of enlightenment are usually only momentary, but those moments are all the more precious, for they lift your vision to higher frequencies.

THE
MINOR
ARCANA

BIRTH OF FIRE
Ace of Wands

BIRTH OF FIRE

ACE OF WANDS

*Keywords: the birth and utilising of new ideas,
igniting the inner fire, discovering hidden strength.*

Louhi had stolen the heavenly lights and hidden them in the
Stone-hill of Pohjola. Darkness consumed the world until
Ukko, the god of weather and sky, grew tired of living without

light. He struck the fire-spark with his sword, a mottled snake and three feathers of the fiery eagle. The fire-spark plunged through the nine heavenly layers, rent asunder the clouds and burned the lands and forests, finally rolling into the lake of Alue, which burst into flames. A pike ate the spark. Väinämöinen heard the pike's cries of pain and called to his aid the folk of the water and a small black man rose from the sea on his behest. Though small he had the strength of many, and he managed to catch the burning fish. Out of the fish came the fire-spark, which the small man gave to Väinämöinen. But the fire-spark broke free again and raged through the land causing devastation. Väinämöinen laboured with the aid of Ilmarinen to recapture it, and was finally able to harness the spark for mankind to use.

MESSAGE: The small man from the sea undertakes the most difficult tasks, and he symbolises the grit within you. The fire-spark represents new, creative realisations, some kind of new way to handle situations. The birth of an idea on a higher level being utilised on a concrete level is portrayed by the fire-spark plunging down through the heavenly layers. The lake of Alue symbolises emotions, and the fact that it is set aflame may mean deep purification and renewal of emotional energies. The unification of fire and water is an alchemical event representing deep inner change. A new kind of energy is waking inside you, bringing light to the darkness. Harnessing that energy may require hard work, but it's sure to be worth it.

BIRTH OF IRON
Two of Wands

BIRTH OF IRON

TWO OF WANDS

*Keywords: bold initiatives, refinement
of ideas, attentiveness, progress.*

Iron was born in heaven when three goddesses of nature milked their breasts and the milk fell to earth. The first one's milk was black, the second white, and the third mixed with blood.

Iron was the youngest of three brothers, Water being the eldest and Fire, the middle one. Fire was going to burn Iron, so Iron hid in the bog. Ilmarinen found Iron there and took it to his smithy where he melted it in his forge, until the ore begged to be released from the searing heat. In its distress Iron swore an oath that it would never cut its brothers or turn against humans. The smelted Iron was still to be hardened, and a honeybee flew in to help Ilmarinen. He asked it to fetch some mead for the quenching water, but a hornet also heard his request. It brought him the anger of adders and the grudge of toads, and Ilmarinen, thinking the honeybee had brought them, added them to the water. Iron became enraged, and has shed blood ever since.

MESSAGE: This card urges you to take responsibility for your own actions. Anger and strife lead to fights and even to wars. There are ways by which conflict can be averted and peace preserved. Pride and self-centredness are the qualities that make one turn the iron against others. This card calls for cooperation and respect for others. You have in your hands something precious you can develop further. Your idea could be made into almost anything, as long as you create yourself the right kind of environment to hone it further. Don't settle for poor options; cast them back into the flames and develop them. This card may also represent cruelty and harm, which the hornet symbolises. Try to surround yourself with loving and encouraging people.

BLIND MAN'S GUIDE
Three of Wands

BLIND MAN'S GUIDE

THREE OF WANDS

Keywords: inner guide, trust, intuition, courage.

According to folklore, some blind people had an astounding ability that allowed them to tread their path with confident steps and to avert any obstacles. The blind would wander in the woods and always find their way back home. One old man forgot his smoking gear in the forest, and was able to find his way to the exact tree stump where he left it. The guide that showed these blind folks their way was a spirit that took the form of a white rabbit, a dog or a ball of fire. But one wasn't allowed to talk about the spirit or it would vanish. An old blind man was so adept at wandering in the woods that a man came from a neighbouring village to see him. The visitor got the old man drunk, and the poor gaffer told him how a white rabbit always hopped before him and all he had to do was follow it. After this the rabbit didn't appear anymore.

MESSAGE: Inner guidance is like the ability to see in a dark forest. It is based on the trust that you will find your way even without knowing what the destination is, or how to get there. Picture a flight of stairs where you can always see the next step. You don't have to know where the stairs end before you've ascended them. You don't need to know what the third step is like before you've climbed the first and second. Obstacles may be met on the path of life, but they can be averted by listening to your instincts. Have faith in your own path and your inner guidance. Stay open to guidance that may manifest from sudden inspiration, a guiding dream, a strange incident or by you simply being in the right place at the right time.

SWIDDEN OF VÄINÄMÖINEN
Four of Wands

SWIDDEN OF VÄINÄMÖINEN

FOUR OF WANDS

Keywords: clearing away obstacles, labour, old replaced by new, freedom from limitations, more fertile ground

When the Sampo fell into the sea and shattered, the waves carried some of its fragments to a shore, where Väinämöinen found them. He took them to the misty headland to grow, but then a tit sang from a tree that crop wouldn't grow if the ground wasn't burned first. Väinämöinen cleared away all vegetation expect for one great birch, which he left so that the birds would have some place to rest. An eagle came and thanked Väinämöinen for sparing the tree as a resting place for the smaller birds and as a throne for the eagle himself. The eagle was so pleased that it repaid Väinämöinen's kindness by igniting the fire he needed to burn his swidden. Once the fire had made the ground fertile for cultivation, Väinämöinen sowed the seeds. He spoke the words of sowing and asked for rain from Ukko, the god of thunder and rain. Ukko allowed the rain to fall, and the barley began to grow.

MESSAGE: Slash-and-burn agriculture involves the field being burned before ploughing and sowing to free nutrients into the soil, making the ground more hospitable for crops to grow. Symbolically this represents the destroying, cleansing and renewing power of fire. This card also refers to the complete purification and renewal of thoughts. Sometimes it's necessary to hack away old ways of thinking, so something new may grow. Set yourself free from the chains of the past and renew your life boldly in a direction that supports your spiritual growth and allows you to express yourself creatively. In relationships this card may symbolise the destruction of presumptions, procedures and power struggles. A more constructive interaction may be growing. Dare to renew your relationships with the consuming and healing power of fire! Good relationships will only get better as the needle thickets burn away.

LEMPO
Five of Wands

LEMPO

FIVE OF WANDS

*Keywords: sexual attraction, infatuation,
charms of love, renewal of feelings.*

In Finnish, one word for love is *lempi*. Lempo was a creature that possessed people with love and temptation. Often cast as a bad creature for bringing unwanted love, Lempo was seen as a threat for legal marriages. The purpose of a love charm was to make the desired bride or groom fall madly in love. Sages cast these sorts of charms, but the common folk also had their own ways. Love charms could be cancelled with counter charms. If someone hadn't had any luck in love, it was possible that he or she was burdened by *luhka*. This was a curse someone had placed upon their victim, and it was invisible to others except sages. Luhka made others look down on that person as a potential spouse and it could only be removed by a sage of the opposite sex.

MESSAGE: This card promises love-filled times, infatuations and perhaps even a new companion. Arrows of love may give birth to fiery emotions when finding their mark. For those already taken, Lempo may strike a new spark to your relationship or it could mean a third party temptation. If you have constant bad luck in your love affairs, it may be the fault of luhka. This invisible repellent could be caused by unresolved feelings of old disappointments. You may repeat, without knowing, old behavioural models. Low self-esteem and a negative attitude or unrealistic bouts of jealousy may also drive people away from you. Fortunately luhka can be removed by dealing with and then letting go of negative experiences. The more you love and respect yourself, the more appealing you'll be in the eyes of others. Luhka may also have been formed from unrealistic expectations towards your companion. The things that make us fall for someone are usually the qualities hiding within ourselves.

FIREFOX
Six of Wands

FIREFOX

SIX OF WANDS

Keywords: vigilance, keen power of
observation, conforming, right timing.

The firefox was a mythical animal whose fur burned with a blue
or green flame. According to folklore, the northern lights were
born when a firefox ran on the mountains of Lapland, and its

fur brushed against trees. Firefox was a prized quarry among huntsmen, for it was believed that whoever managed to catch it would become rich and famous. The fox's fur was also valued merchandise on its own. There seems to be unexplainable magic in the wondrous phenomenon of the northern lights that makes time stand still for a moment. In olden times, the northern lights were used to tell people's fortunes, and they were both respected and feared. The Sami people took the bells from their reindeers' necks when the northern lights appeared, and the women didn't go out without covering their heads. They also believed the northern lights to be the winter equivalent for thunderstorms, and that both were created when fire and water mixed. In their own way, the northern lights were alive and aware, and according to folklore, whistling and hollering while they were burning.

MESSAGE: The fox is the cunning trickster of fairy tales who smells opportunities and is always one step ahead. A swift, intelligent animal, firefox advises you to look before you leap. Its strength is based on its ability to sense opportunities and dangers, and it knows when to grab the moment and when to steer clear. It takes vigilance and luck to see the northern lights. They offer a wondrous moment that pauses the daily grind for a spell, and their beauty may lead to a deep inner inspiration and the fire of creativity. This card promises fortune and success in your endeavours. It may also symbolise the growth of material or spiritual wealth or unexpected lucky strikes. Remain vigilant so opportunities won't slip by.

WOLF'S BRIDE
Seven of Wands

WOLF'S BRIDE

SEVEN OF WANDS

*Keywords: courage, open-mindedness, yearning
for freedom, taking the crucial step.*

The Wolf's Bride is a novel by Finnish author Aino Kallas. The novel, set in Estonia in the 1600s, tells the story of Aalo, who is turned into a werewolf. She was the Wolf's Bride who heard the call of her kind, and the great spirit of the woodlands took control of her soul and body. At nights she left her husband's side and abandoned her small child to run with her pack. Her yearning for freedom grew with every transformation, and in the end she forgot her human life completely. She couldn't resist her inner calling; it overwhelmed her mind and forced her to trust in her instincts, without caring about the consequences. She was a rebel who abandoned her community's narrow-minded views of how she should live her life to follow her own inner truth. Even though Aalo was burned at the stake, it didn't make her a better or worse person than anyone else. She didn't seek the wolves' company out of spite, but to be who she truly was.

MESSAGE: This card challenges you to be who you truly are without caring what others think. It also warns not to judge others because they are different. This kind of behaviour is not guided by love or acceptance but fear towards all things different. Humans are by their nature afraid of everything that is unknown or beyond comprehension or sight. Pioneers like the Wolf's Bride strive to turn the unknown into the known, to dissipate fear and put themselves on the line without being afraid of the consequences. As a reward for this courage and open-mindedness they get to experience something that will forever remain out of reach for those who are judgemental and controlled by fear. May courage be your life's strength. Trust your own instinct.

SAUNA
Eight of Wands

SAUNA

EIGHT OF WANDS

Keywords: healing, relaxation, sacred state,
physical and spiritual purification.

One of the most important symbols of Finnish identity is the sauna. The person who first set fire in a new sauna's stove was believed to become the sauna's guardian spirit after his death.

It was customary to warm up the sauna just for its spirit a few times a year and no one else was allowed to bathe at that time. Sometimes food was taken to the sauna as an offering for the dead members of the family. A sauna was also the place where children were born, the sick healed and the dead prepared for their burial. The word *löyly* doesn't only mean the steam rising from the sauna's stove. Löyly is one of the oldest Finno-Ugric words and it means one of the three souls of a person. Löyly determined the length of every human's life, from the first breath to the last, which was when löyly departed. A difficult and drawn-out death was hastened by opening the stove's damper, so that löyly could leave more easily for the afterlife. The second part was called *itse*, which had to do with social life. The soul's third part was *henki*, spirit.

MESSAGE: This card refers to the need to separate oneself from the daily grind, and to give yourself time to just be warm and relaxed. Your strength will restore and your mind will invigorate, and then you can resume your tasks with joy and a positive attitude. Something new is approaching in your life, and it is wise to calm down before it arrives. A sauna is the best place to meditate and calm down. Both body and mind are purified, and the overall feeling is of renewal afterwards. The mind calms down and solutions are found as if by themselves. Leave your worries behind, and relax for a while.

GOLDEN BRIDE
Nine of Wands

GOLDEN BRIDE

NINE OF WANDS

Keywords: disappointment, delusions,
unrealistic expectations, compassion.

Smith Ilmarinen had married the Maid of Pohjola and settled down with her, and it soon became clear that she could be as mean as she was beautiful. Kullervo, Ilmarinen's servant, had a falling out with her, and she baked a stone inside his bread. The only thing Kullervo owned was a knife that had belonged to his father. The knife's blade broke against the hidden stone when he tried to cut the bread, and this enraged him. He cursed the Maid of Pohjola, and called forth wolves and bears that devoured Ilmarinen's livestock. Then he made the beasts appear as slaughtered cows, and when the Maid came to milk them, they killed her. Ilmarinen mourned his lost wife, and in the end forged himself a new spouse from gold and silver. But a woman made from cold, hard metal was of no comfort to him, and finally Ilmarinen grew tired of his golden bride. He tried to give it to Väinämöinen, but the old sage was terrified of the metal monstrosity, and told Ilmarinen to cast it back to the forge and destroy it.

MESSAGE: There is no such thing as a perfect human; everyone has both good and bad qualities. Ilmarinen forged the woman of his dreams but it was a lifeless, inhuman thing. The Maid had turned out to be evil and heartless, quite the opposite of the picture Ilmarinen had of her. The Maid didn't bother to be kind to Kullervo, but mistreated him in her pride and contempt. We should not judge others based on their situation or outer qualities. The deductions and stories we make about others are never the whole truth. Learn to discern the truth from lies before you make deductions. Practise compassion and try to see the good qualities even in your enemies.

THE DRAGON
Ten of Wands

THE DRAGON

TEN OF WANDS

*Keywords: will to fight back, courage,
freedom from fears, warrior.*

It was told that dragons had a hypnotic gaze used to petrify
their victim, and they could read minds, shape-shift and confuse
a person's vision. It was said the dragons' source of power was

a mythical stone, drakontia, which was lodged in their heads, and feverishly sought after by the alchemists of the middle-ages. Drakontia was said to be the pivotal ingredient of the life-elixir that could cure any disease and grant eternal life. Dragons belonged to the realm of monsters where mortals couldn't enter without being singed. The stories often place dragons in a perilous field of jagged rocks or a fortress than can be compared to the afterlife, where they guard their treasure. Some stories say dragons were originally evil and greedy humans who wouldn't allow their riches to be inherited and spent, but rather buried them. After their deaths they were transformed into dragons, so that they could continue to guard their wealth.

MESSAGE: The dragon represents courage and strength. You are like a warrior able to surmount any danger or challenge. You believe in yourself and your abilities, and you defend your treasures fiercely when need be. You won't agree to compromise or being controlled. You may be tested in different ways but you won't give up. You will fight bravely against opposing forces and clear your way out of suffocating situations, and be victorious. The battle may be draining, but the treasure will be yours in the end and it will be worth all the trouble. This card reminds you the only direction is forwards. Arise again and again, every time more complete, stronger. You are courageous, you can do anything. The dragon may also represent the fear of destruction. Do not give in to your fears, but bravely face even the most challenging situations.

THE EAGLE
Page of Wands

THE EAGLE

PAGE OF WANDS

Keywords: highest consciousness, broadened vision,
new perspective, surmounting challenges, rescue.

The eagle had a fiery mouth and its eyes gleamed with flames.
Also called 'thunderbird', it was the companion of Ukko, the god
of thunder. Using eagle feathers, Ukko stoked the first fire that

was plunged down to earth for mankind to use. A fiery eagle on a flaming birch's crown, ready to rend asunder anyone who tried to pass, was the first obstacle on the path to the afterlife. Fiery birds, such as the phoenix, are met in different mythologies all over the world. Rebirth and renewing are the cleansing properties of fire, when old things turn to ashes to make way for new. The eagle appears also as a saviour and benefactor in the *Kalevala*. An eagle helps Väinämöinen to ignite the fire which burns the first swidden. Ilmarinen forged a fiery eagle which aided him to catch a pike from the black river of Tuonela. During the raid of Sampo, Louhi transformed herself into an eagle.

MESSAGE: The eagle represents broad vision and objectivity. From high above it can easily comprehend the bigger picture. Symbolising higher consciousness, broad perspective and courage to have faith in yourself and your strength, the fiery eagle also represents the light of consciousness and keen perception. Its strength and speed make it a powerful ally. When Louhi turned herself into an eagle, she rose above the situation and turned it to her own advantage by ascending to a higher level of consciousness. Inspect your situation from a broader perspective. Distance yourself from day-to-day worries by focusing on longer term plans. The eagle urges you to understand the situation as clearly as possible, and then to look further. In the *Kalevala*, an eagle always comes to the rescue when the situation is looking grim. This card may also refer to a change of direction.

THE HORSE OF HIISI
Knight of Wands

THE HORSE OF HIISI

KNIGHT OF WANDS

*Keywords: taking on challenges, taking risks,
harnessing the power of the mind.*

Louhi, the Mistress of Pohjola, gave three tasks to her daughters'
suitors, and the second that was given to Lemminkäinen was to
harness the Horse of Hiisi. Lemminkäinen climbed a great hill

and saw a brown, fiery-maned steed in the east. He called upon the god of thunder and a storm broke out; water, ice and hail rained upon the horse smothering its flames. Lemminkäinen promised to be kind to it if it would allow itself to be harnessed, and the horse complied. Lemminkäinen slipped the harness over its head and rode to Pohjola to claim his prize. Louhi wasn't satisfied with the suitors' abilities though, and ordered Lemminkäinen to shoot the Swan of Tuonela as his final task. Finnish sages have also utilised mythical horses when banishing ailments. They would call a horse from Hiisi which would then carry the illness, curse or whatever to the caverns of the great Stone-hill of Pohjola.

MESSAGE: To reach his goal, Lemminkäinen controlled his fiery temperament and gained more power in everything he did. He knew how to direct his strength towards the target, and progressed successfully from one challenge to another. This card is saying you have the necessary strength to attain your objective. You will advance with speed surmounting all obstacles coming your way. This card represents control over instincts and urges and directing them to fruitful targets. You will also need clear methods, creative power and original thinking to bend the Horse of Hiisi to your will. You have a mission and will succeed in it. The card also urges you not to be blinded by success. Vain pride and rash actions may pull everything apart in seconds. You may have avoided facing your dark side and challenges thus far, but now you're ready to head straight into the fire!

MOTHER OF FIRE
Queen of Wands

MOTHER OF FIRE

QUEEN OF WANDS

*Keywords: self-knowledge, warmth,
wellbeing, continuity, loving.*

The mother of fire lived in the stove's ashes or behind the oven,
sometimes appearing as a figure in the hearth's flames. It could
live in any fireplace in a building, and its purpose was to protect

the fire. It could, for example, wake the inhabitants and warn them if fire was about to break out. The mother of fire appeared the moment the first fire was ignited in a fireplace. It was believed the first person to set the fire would become the house's spirit upon dying, so it was carefully considered who got to do it to ensure the house would get the best possible spirit. As the spirit brought good fortune, people would take it with them when moving to a new place by taking ash from three different spots of the old hearth to the new one. Fire-spirits needed to be respected for they could become so enraged they burned the house down. Fire worship has its roots in primitive ages when fire and hearth were sacred. Tales were exchanged around the fire, strengthening a community's feeling of togetherness.

MESSAGE: The hearth has always been the symbol of the spiritual centre of a home. The upward rising smoke symbolises prayers addressed to the gods above. This card tells of caring, warmth, contentment and safety among family members and close friends around the home, and good fortune in family relationships and at home. But no fire burns if it's not taken care of. This card advises you to cherish love and close relationships. Express your feelings openly with your loved ones. This card also suggests you've achieved deep self-knowledge through the adversities you have faced. You can relax and concentrate on your inner world. Your compassion has grown thanks to your experiences, and you're able to face people with gentleness.

PANU
King of Wands

PANU

KING OF WANDS

Keywords: virility, passion, creativity, strong will.

Panu was the spirit of fire and also the son of the sun. Providing light, warmth and protection against predators, it also symbolised a human's inner fire, ideas and creativity. Fire is a cleansing element that may also be a source of great calamity in the wrong hands. Fire was considered a living creature never to be befouled with trash or disturbed in vain. One could take the forces of fire with them by taking ash from a root burned by a forest fire with their knife and placing it in a clean cloth. According to folklore, the forces of fire were seen as a sort of lightning before special events, when help was needed. The crackling fire and smoke of the juniper were used to banish harmful spirits and ailments. The mysterious sounds the burning fire made were known as the language of fire, and if a person became wise to it, they would become the fire's master able to put it out and whom flames couldn't hurt. It was believed that the thoughts that occurred when a fire crackled would become true.

MESSAGE: Panu represents burning feelings and passions. The king of the fire folks may also indicate someone who is passionate yet stable, with an equal amount of consideration and daring. With this kind of inner fire, a person may achieve great things in life, but others may consider them selfish. This is incorrect, for they are merely strong, ready to boldly seize challenges. Success is sure to follow, and it's not always easy for others to see the labour behind the triumph. This card urges you to realise your own solutions with greater confidence and to trust in your own abilities. Be proud of your accomplishments. Panu may also warn about overly intense passions, jealousy and fanaticism.

TOAST OF UKKO
Ace of Cups

TOAST OF UKKO

ACE OF CUPS

*Keywords: abundance, gratitude, respecting
the forces of nature, fertility.*

Ukko was worshipped as the giver of rain and fertility, and the
Ukko celebrations were customarily held after the spring sowing
and in drought. The people gathered at the field's shoulder to

raise a toast for Ukko. The point of the sacrificial ritual was that it would look favourable in Ukko's eyes, and the god of rain would then water the fields. Generally the toast was ale, but a swig of spirit was also acceptable, and people were most likely intoxicated during the celebration. It was also customary to sprinkle some of the toast in the air, as symbolical raindrops. The sacrificial offerings, such as spirits and ale, were taken to a high rock that was called the mountain of Ukko. The point of these gifts was to prevent the summer from being too dry. Ukko also received some of the food that had been prepared for the celebration.

MESSAGE: This card is linked to ensuring continuity and to developing abundance. Merriment and celebration are an integral part of the Toast of Ukko in honouring the forces of nature. This card tells you that what you've sowed will grow with the aid of invigorating rains. Sowing symbolises the planting of new ideas, new projects and spiritual growth. The Toast of Ukko is a symbol of giving love that unites that which is above to that which is below, and reaches deep into the ground, causing fertile and plentiful growth on both physical and spiritual levels. This card is also about love for oneself, and remembering the most plentiful fount of love resides in a person's core. Giving love requires no effort, for an endless and constant bounty is flowing to us, as long as we remain open and receptive. The rain washes clean, refreshes and invigorates.

SPRING SPIRIT
Two of Cups

SPRING SPIRIT

TWO OF CUPS

*Keywords: living in the moment,
friendship, mental clarity.*

Spring spirits were translucent beings living in fresh, pure waters
that welled from the depths of the earth. These beings never
harboured unpleasant thoughts; their minds were always clear

and untainted. They were sensitive and benevolent, ethereal beings who lived in the moment and could transform themselves into droplets glimmering in the colours of the rainbow. They existed for pure joy, bestowing health and wellbeing; it was believed a dip into water guarded by such a spirit could make all ailments disappear. Pikes and frogs were kept in wells in the days of yore, as a spirit animal to keep the water clean. In Sweden it was customary to use eels for the same purpose; the oldest well-eel ever found was 155 years old. The thought of a lonely fish going around in circles in a dark well is a sad, depressing one. A person that wasn't making any progress or getting anywhere would sometimes be playfully called a 'well-eel'.

MESSAGE: Springs were thought to be gateways to deeper levels of consciousness. This card may symbolise the deepening of a romantic relationship; it also indicates balanced and harmonious relationships that increase your wellbeing. Treasure them and spend time with those you love. This card may also mean healing on an emotional level, and regaining joy in life. Feelings hide in the depths of the well. The water in the 'well' of a happy and content person is clear. They have the courage to express themselves sincerely. But if the water is murky, a person can feel depressed. An empty well symbolises spiritual exhaustion. If you feel yourself to be as lonely as a well-eel, then bravely step out of your comfort zone. The eel is ready to travel long distances to natural breeding grounds. The card urges you to head towards new adventures.

KANTELE OF VÄINÄMÖINEN

Three of Cups

KANTELE OF VÄINÄMÖINEN

THREE OF CUPS

*Keywords: sense of community, harmony with
all creation, communication at heart level.*

When Väinämöinen, Ilmarinen and Lemminkäinen were on
their way to retrieve the Sampo from Pohjola, their boat ran
aground on the back of a gigantic pike. When Väinämöinen

plunged his sword through the pike and lifted it, it tore in half. The tail sank back into the sea but the head fell into the boat. The travellers went ashore to make food out of it, and Väinämöinen took the jawbone and fashioned it into the first kantele of Kalevala. When he began to play, people gathered and every four-legged creature of the forest hurried to listen. Tapio, lord of the forest, climbed onto a hill and Mielikki, mistress of the forest, onto a birch to listen to the sweet melody. All the birds, even the mighty eagle, flew to hear the music. Maids of Air listened on their rainbow. Ahti, lord of water, sat on a lily pad. Maids of Vellamo ceased to comb their hair. Vellamo, mother of water, rose onto a rock. All wept from joy. Even Väinämöinen himself wept into the sea and his tears became pearls.

MESSAGE: Väinämöinen's joy and surrender when playing his kantele can't be forced. Life's hardships have cultivated a deep harmony and wisdom within him, and they are uniting with a sensitive, intuitive and creative way of expressing feelings. Väinämöinen is the mature, experienced part of you – your wise, inner guide. He managed to slay the great pike and also invent the kantele, and he turned out to be a natural talent whose music brought joy to the whole of creation. Believe in your talents. Turning unexpected situations into victories is also part of this card's theme. There's no reason to panic or abandon all hope if the boat gets stuck. Your situation is solvable, and it may result in surprising new possibilities on your path.

IKU-TURSO
Four of Cups

IKU-TURSO

FOUR OF CUPS

*Keywords: self-examination, facing the shadows of the
past and being freed from fear, change for the better.*

When the men of Kalevala had stolen the Sampo from Pohjola
and were trying to flee in their boat, Louhi called the sea monster
Iku-Turso from the depths to stop them. When the sea began to

churn as the monster rose from the waves, Ilmarinen hid under a cover, but Väinämöinen had more courage. He leaned over, grasped Iku-Turso by its ears and demanded to know why it had arisen to hinder them. Iku-Turso refused to answer until Väinämöinen asked for the third time. Then it admitted it had risen in order to kill the men of Kalevala and return the Sampo to Pohjola. Väinämöinen forbade the monster from rising to the surface ever again, and ever since, the Iku-Turso hasn't bothered humans.

MESSAGE: Something strange has tangled itself in your net: water plants or weeds, some creature of the deep, eyes and hands that grasp at the oars and sides of your boat. You'll be stuck until you clear this mess. Water is the element of feelings; there might well be unfinished business hiding in the depths, something from your past needing to be solved. Listen to yourself: why has Iku-Turso snatched you? What is holding you? Fears and past disappointments beneath the surface are coming into your consciousness, and manifesting through your emotions and thoughts. This card refers to old inner demons that may be your own unpleasant characteristics, past incidents in relationships, and wrong choices that you've been trying to hide from yourself. A mere change in attitude and deeper examination of oneself is often enough to solve this situation. It is good to say out loud what you are afraid of and to look at unpleasant things right in the eye. To face a fear is to rob it of its power.

WILL O' THE WISP
Five of Cups

WILL O' THE WISP

FIVE OF CUPS

Keywords: hopes, boredom, getting lost in feelings, unfulfilled expectations.

Will o' the wisps were ethereal lights seen at graveyards, bogs or the surfaces of lakes at nighttime. They resembled greenish or bluish flames that could move from place to place and suddenly vanish. A moving will o' the wisp was also thought to be a lantern that some creature carried through the darkness. It was also believed they marked the places of hidden treasure and the hidden treasure could be discovered if a person happened to come across it at the precise, magical moment when the will o' the wisp was burning. Will o' the wisps were especially numerous during the night of Midsummer's day. These fickle flames could get those who followed them lost, but if treated right, they could also lead lost people back to the right path.

MESSAGE: Will o' the wisp's message relates to chasing an unattainable dream or fancy. The human mind can lose itself in the world of utopian fantasies, preventing ideas from becoming concrete. If we catch up to a will o' the wisp, it will simply vanish. One cannot capture these lights, just as one cannot capture happiness or love. This card refers to an attitude in which happiness is achieved when something is attained or completed. Happiness is an intrinsic feeling; as long as we think it to be in some external thing, we will always feel like it's missing. This card urges you to live here and now. It may also symbolise how you've already grown tired of something that previously was a source of pleasure for you. This card can also mean you are chasing something you cannot get or something you've lost. Unfulfilled expectations lead to disappointment. Experience prepares you for something even better than that which you hoped to find beneath the will o' the wisp.

BOG SPIRIT
Six of Cups

BOG SPIRIT

SIX OF CUPS

Keywords: mire of feelings, exhaustion,
uncertainty, caution.

According to folklore, on the path to the afterlife there was
a great bog where sinners sank under the weight of their bad
deeds. It was a terrifying place – a limbo at the threshold of

two worlds, not quite water, not quite land. Greenish lights, believed to be will o' the wisps, were sometimes seen in the bog, burning over buried treasures which were sacrifices to the dead or valuables hidden from enemies. Bog spirits kept guard of the bog ponds that were gateways to the lower layers of the world. These spirits were the great healers who could banish diseases into the bog with healing spells. The bog also gave bog ore or iron ore. Iron originated from the heavens and when its brother Fire burned it, Iron hid in the bog ponds. Later Iron came forth when bears and wolves ran over the bog, and the ore rose into their paw prints with herbs that had iron in them.

MESSAGE: The bog may be a sign of sinking, emotional ground where it is dangerous to travel. Bog spirit urges you to consider your next step carefully. It may also warn of uncertainty, fear or stagnation. Bravely seek new ways to confront your problems, and don't let anything disperse your energies. There's no sense in sinking into a bog pond voluntarily. You may need to rest and wait until you feel better. The bog spirit may also warn you of relationships that consume more energy than they provide. Everyone must take the responsibility for their own lives and all of its mires. Take care to keep your feet on dry land, and do not let people playing the victim bother you. You may aid those close to you but you cannot save them unless they are willing to fight to get back on solid ground.

NIXIE
Seven of Cups

NIXIE

SEVEN OF CUPS

*Keywords: falseness, prejudices, discovering
the truth, misunderstandings.*

Nixie was a creature that lived in almost every Finnish body
of water, stalking its prey in wells, on beaches and in rapids.
It tricked people into water to drown them. A nixie could

assume any form, taking the shape it thought would please the unknowing victim. It sometimes appeared as a rock that tempted people to swim to it. Nixie was used as a bogeyman to keep children from going near water alone, lest it catch them. Talented violinists, nixies also taught this skill. According to folklore one could seek this teacher out by going to a large rock in a rapid and playing there during some magical moment, like the night of Midsummer's day. The nixie would insist pupils gird themselves to it with a belt, to prevent them from falling into the water. It was imperative not to buckle the belt though, or else the nixie would pull the player underwater after the lesson was over.

MESSAGE: Nixie refers to misunderstandings and falsehood. Something is not what it seems to be. What is the real motivation behind an action or speech? Trust your intuition and don't allow yourself to be led by others. Rumours, gossip and expectations may make it difficult to form an objective opinion of a situation. This card may also suggest you are not seeing things clearly. You may be telling yourself stories you believe are right, but in fact, they are not. Your thoughts of a situation or a person might not be the whole truth. Seek for more facts before you make an opinion. Nixie will lose its power when it's recognised and its name is said. It is the same with fears, prejudices and misunderstandings. They too lose their power when recognised. Trust the truth you feel is right in your heart.

VORTEX
Eight of Cups

VORTEX

EIGHT OF CUPS

*Keywords: destination, change of course, chaotic
feelings, finding a deeper meaning in life.*

At the farthest reaches of the Arctic Ocean, where the world's
edge was believed to be, there was a gigantic vortex that
swallowed everything that came near. It was also the gateway

to the underworld, the kingdom of Manala, ruled by demonic forces and where the spirits of the dead were believed to go. Shamans also used it when travelling between the world's layers. The passage that opened inside the vortex was believed to go all the way to the other side of the world, where another vortex spat out the water the other one had swallowed. The same path led from the vortex's mouth upward to the heavenly layers, through which the world column that held the heavens led. The vortex also plays a part in the *Kalevala*'s ending. After a virgin gives birth to a child, Väinämöinen baptises the boy as the new king of Karelia. He announces it is his time to stand aside and give way to the younger generation, and sets sail towards the vortex where he descends to the kingdom of the underworld. Väinämöinen's departure is a symbolical representation of old pagan religions yielding to the new Christianity.

MESSAGE: Vortex symbolises the gateway to the underworld and the subconscious levels of the mind, and suggests something has disrupted the flow of the current. Collisions, tensions and conflicts may rear their heads in your situation. There is danger of getting drawn to even deeper waters. It is time to take a good look at where you are heading in your life. Are you the captain of your boat or are you floating around where the current takes you? Take control of and responsibility for your life. Choose your direction and head towards it. Väinämöinen represents your wise, inner guide to whom the card urges you to listen.

RAPID SPIRIT
Nine of Cups

RAPID SPIRIT

NINE OF CUPS

Keywords: powerful progress, focus,
facing and conquering challenges.

Väinämöinen, Ilmarinen and Lemminkäinen were on their way
to Pohjola to get the Sampo. Väinämöinen had found a boat
on the shore and turned it into a mighty warship. When the

boat entered into a rapid, Lemminkäinen began to chant the words of rafting, calling the rapid spirits to help by smoothing the stones into moss and spinning a blue yarn to mark the safe path, which the rapid spirits did. According to the Finnish folklore, these were the most powerful spirits of the water. It was dangerous to offend them, for they could claim their revenge by drowning people. One such spirit became enraged when a mill was built into its rapid, and one foggy December morn, the spirit unleashed a flood so great that the mill and some of the houses built close to the shore were washed away.

MESSAGE: The power in the rapids' wild torrents pushes you forward. In the right hands this energy can produce miracles. The thrust of the rapids are driving you forward with such force that you must just focus on finishing the task at hand. The torrents will calm in time, and so can you. Give your full attention to those tasks you feel most attracted to. Your direction is the right one. Ilmarinen, Väinämöinen and Lemminkäinen represent the forces within you that you will need on your journey. Old Väinämöinen symbolises the wisdom you've gained from life experiences. Lemminkäinen symbolises courage and the ability to throw oneself into life without fear for the challenges it will bring. Smith Ilmarinen symbolises the skill with which you can express the talents and possibilities within you. By using all these powers in your situation, you have a great chance of making it through the challenges ahead with success.

THE PIKE OF TUONELA
Ten of Cups

THE PIKE OF TUONELA

TEN OF CUPS

Keywords: great chance, final challenge,
breakthrough, success.

Ilmarinen proposed to the Maid of Pohjola, and her mother, Louhi, gave him tasks to prove his worthiness. Ilmarinen had already forged the Sampo but Louhi still demanded one final feat of skill from her future son-in-law. He was to catch the gigantic pike of Tuonela without using any tools. The Maid of Pohjola had begun to fancy Ilmarinen and helped the smith in his tasks; she also advised him how to catch the fish. She prompted Ilmarinen to forge a fiery eagle to catch the pike for him. Ilmarinen took her advice and fashioned an eagle that so gargantuan that when one of its wings reached the heavens, the other touched the ground. The eagle and pike fought to the death. The pike slipped through the eagle's talons, but on the third try, the bird managed to lift its opponent from the water and flew away. The giant pike's head was left to Ilmarinen, and he took it to Pohjola for Louhi to use as a throne. The Mistress of Pohjola was finally convinced of the suitor's worthiness and agreed to give him her daughter. The Wedding of Pohjola was held soon after.

MESSAGE: Catching the huge fish is like a dream come true; it might mean hard work and persistence but it's worth it. This card urges you to take on the challenges at hand. Your efforts will be rewarded. Ilmarinen finally got the sought-after Maid of Pohjola as his bride. The eagle symbolises higher powers, high consciousness and clear perception. Louhi's tasks represent the challenges you face in life. By using his talent and skills Ilmarinen was finally able to reach his goal, which the Maid of Pohjola symbolises. The pike's head acted as a trophy, symbolising governing position and mastery.

AINO
Page of Cups

AINO

PAGE OF CUPS

*Keywords: following your inner truth, setting
boundaries, self-confidence, independent thinking.*

Young Joukahainen had sought to challenge Väinämöinen to
a duel of knowledge, but the old sage defeated his opponent
without effort, and sang him into a bog. To save himself,

Joukahainen promised his sister to Väinämöinen. When the poor girl learned of the bargain her brother had struck with him, she ran crying to her mother, but her mother was delighted to get Väinämöinen as her son-in-law. No one cared what Aino had to say. In her desperation, Aino thought she would rather drown than give herself to Väinämöinen. She saw three maids bathing in the sea, and joined them. She sat on a rock and it disappeared beneath the waves and took her with it down to the watery kingdom. Väinämöinen mourned her deeply. He took his fishing rod to the sea, and on the third day he caught a fish he had never seen anything like before. The fish freed itself and swam further away, where it appeared as a beautiful maid, and chastised Väinämöinen for not recognising she was Aino. Väinämöinen cursed his rotten luck for letting her get away a second time.

MESSAGE: Aino's fate is a heartbreaking tale of a soul's yearning for freedom. Aino chose freedom in the mermaids' merry company against the expectations of her family and Väinämöinen. Thus she maintained the purity of her soul and spirit. Remain true to yourself and to your feelings. Defend your freedom. Aino may warn you of relationships in which giving and receiving are not in balance. Make sure that the choices are your own and that they feel right. If a promise you've given doesn't feel right, then it probably isn't. Don't do anything that doesn't truly feel good. Don't compromise in your emotional life. Your life is yours to control, no one else's.

VETEHINEN
Knight of Cups

VETEHINEN

KNIGHT OF CUPS

*Keywords: quick reactions, control over
emotional needs, swift action.*

Vetehinens were male water spirits whose sphere of influence
included lakes and ponds. Sometimes the spirits of different lakes
could end up in a fight, and the lakes' waters would start to splash

so hard, the other lake could dry up entirely. Impulsive, passionate and easily angered spirits, vetehinens liked to keep to themselves. Bad behaviour on the water could incur the spirit's wrath, which would be seen in diminishing catches for fishermen, and it could even have more far-reaching ramifications. If a vetehinen was mocked, it could rise from the water and come demanding the offenders' heads. As long as vetehinens weren't disturbed and people minded their manners on the water, they were benevolent providers of fish. When treated with respect they could even begin to protect the person from the dangers of water and drowning, or give endless fisherman's luck in return. Vetehinens were also skilled foretellers, and it was customary to go at Epiphany to talk to the vetehinen through a hole in the ice about what would happen during the year.

MESSAGE: Vetehinen lords over the world below the surface – the unknown depths of the emotional life. It is good sign that you're swimming in these deep waters, for you are searching for new understanding to your situation by diving bravely into the unknown. Vetehinen represents power which may be rebellious, fickle and sometimes aggressive. This card also symbolises swift action and reactivity. This card urges you to inspect the limits you have set for yourself and learn to face challenges directly. Vetehinen urges you to get to know your dark side and accept all your different aspects. The churning of water may indicate emotions erupting within you. Perhaps you've repressed them deep in your subconscious and denied their existence. Try not to direct them towards other people.

VELLAMO
Queen of Cups

VELLAMO

QUEEN OF CUPS

Keywords: sincerity, love, care, expressiveness.

Vellamo was a female water spirit and the mother of water. Her purpose was to give fish to the fishermen, to keep an eye on the amount of roe, and to protect all the fish species. She was a beautiful, sensitive being who loved all inhabitants of the water, and also gladly helped humans by giving catches to those who asked nicely. Sometimes she would rise from the waves to a rock on the shore to comb her long hair, and if one happened to meet her, it was best to greet her politely, for she may bestow supernatural gifts as a show of gratitude, such as eternal luck in all financial dealings or luck in love. Vellamo liked to linger in calm, clean waters and abhorred pollution and overfishing. Those who disturbed the younglings of waterfowl or broke their eggs would incur her wrath, and she may have tangled offenders' nets and let fish loose from them. Sometimes she grew sorrowful and desperate when trying to free fish ensnared by plastic waste, or when trying to guide schools away from pollution oozing into the waters.

MESSAGE: Vellamo urges you to find balance on an emotional level and represents genuine, harmonious relationships and sensitive feelings shown openly and purely. The clean waters Vellamo governs symbolise emotions and the subconscious, and the fish represent spirituality, inspiration, intuition, instinct and fertility. Fish thrive in clean, balanced waters and Vellamo drives them away from polluted waters which symbolise negative, smothered thoughts and feelings that disrupt a person's spiritual wellbeing. The mother of water is a healer who doesn't judge but gently advises people to search for inner peace and to love themselves and others. A polite, compassionate and sincere approach will bring out the best in everyone you meet.

AHTI
King of Cups

AHTI

KING OF CUPS

Keywords: spiritually important relationships,
clear emotional life, surrendering to loved ones.

Ahti was the king of water, the protector of fishermen and
seafarers. He ruled over all bodies of water and fish, and it was
said he was the forefather of seals. He was asked to provide

luck for fishermen, especially when fishing on a larger scale. His kingdom held all the riches of the seas, and he governed over sunken ships and treasure. Even the Sampo was under Ahti's control, though it shattered into small pieces at the bottom of the sea. His sceptre was powerful, and if he wanted, he could assume the form of a crest of a wave or blend in with the reeds to watch over his kingdom. Sometimes he showed himself to fishermen. If he was in fine clothes and looked benevolent, one could expect a good catch. But the first catch had to be sacrificed to him, preferably before the fisher tasted the catch. All sorts of obscene behaviour, arguing and cursing would anger Ahti. He could be appeased by sacrificing gold and silver into the water.

MESSAGE: The element of water symbolises emotions and family life. A generous, loving and caring father figure, Ahti gives his all to his loved ones, but demands respect and good behaviour in return. His purpose is to ensure the continuation of life, and he protects his community and family. Do you feel you're floating lost on sea, or are you the captain of your own ship? Is the sea calm or stormy? Are your emotions churning or tranquil? Ahti's energy may help you to control your emotions in the changes of life, during its ups and downs, and give courage in different dangers. Allow yourself time to express your own creativity and imagination. Ahti values gold and silver, which symbolise spiritual protection, truth, and the light that comes from higher consciousness.

THE HONEY BEE
Ace of Swords

THE HONEY BEE

ACE OF SWORDS

Keywords: healing, diligence, cooperation, sincerity.

The honeybee was the benevolent helper of Kalevala who flew to aid the Mother of Lemminkäinen as her son lay dead on the banks of the river of Tuonela, and fetched balm to revive him. Lemminkäinen's return from the dead is a tale of the omnipotent power of motherly love that grants women the power to cross the border between life and death. The source of the revitalising balm was a bowl or a spring in the realm of the gods, beneath the world tree at the centre of the world. The keeper of the spring and the world's centre were life-giving, protecting goddesses, the three fates who weaved the inkles of life. When Louhi was preparing the Wedding of Pohjola she summoned the honeybee to help her make the ale, and the honeybee brought the ale to life. It flew through nine layers of heaven to fetch the elixir of life that made the ale ferment. The honeybee's counterpart was the wicked hornet, who brought its own, foul ingredients to Ilmarinen as he was learning how to use iron.

MESSAGE: The honeybee travelled to the afterlife to fetch the life-giving, healing nectar and carried whispered messages to the dead. It is thanks to bees that flowers and fruits are pollinated, producing crops. The honeybee is associated with diligence, industrious labour, altruism and willingness to help. It is also linked to motherly love, warmth and nurture that has a healing effect. In relationships, this card refers to sincere love and friendship, forgiveness and acceptance. Do not worry, for the small bee is trying to help you. You may see how your negative feelings turn into love and your old wounds are healed. The honeybee also signifies that death cannot sever the connection between two souls. You can see your loved ones who have passed on, through your dreams.

FOLK OF LINTUKOTO
Two of Swords

FOLK OF LINTUKOTO

TWO OF SWORDS

*Keywords: search for balance and peace of
mind, dreams, hopes, wanderlust.*

Far in the south, where heaven and earth meet, there was an
opening through which migrating birds flew south for winter.
This far-off land was called Lintukoto, the home of birds, and

its inhabitants were known as the folk of Lintukoto. The Milky Way, known in Finland literally as the 'Bird Track', was thought to show them the way. The folk of Lintukoto lived at the edge of the world. It was believed there was a vast sea between Finland and the warm lands of the south, and only one island in that sea. It was here the migrating birds rested on their journey, including willy wagtails that had ridden on the backs of cranes. Cranes were seen as the migrant birds' leaders with whom the folk of Lintukoto fought because the cranes ate the seeds from thei fields.

MESSAGE: It was always warm and blissful on Lintukoto, there was no shortage of food, and one could relax and calm down. But the journey was a long and arduous one, and so Lintukoto remained just a fantasy for most. After every long, dark winter the migrant birds would return to their home from the land of fortune and bring the summer with them. The wedge of cranes was the sign of nearing spring. This card symbolises dreams of a better place; perhaps you're growing sick of day-to-day routines and a vacation is in order. This card tells of the need for solitude, for a place without worries. Dreams of a better way help you to seek new routes towards a happier life. This card also bears a warning: old troubles have a habit of following you. Facing and solving problems helps you move forward, and that's when the island of the blissful may be found inside of you.

LIEKKIÖ
Three of Swords

LIEKKIÖ

THREE OF SWORDS

Keywords: sorrow, self-blame, doubts, unused possibilities.

Illegitimate children were outcasts of communities in the olden days. The strict norms of society and fear of punishment made some women strive to hide unwanted pregnancies and to kill the child and bury it without being noticed to avoid being ostracised. Usually the child was buried in the woods or beneath the floor of a house. The mother's social status remained the same, but there was no rest for the child who had been denied its chance to live and then buried without being baptised. The child would be bound to the place where its mother had buried it, and would appear as a *liekkiö*, a child ghost that tried to gain the attention of passersby by crying. If a liekkiö was followed, it usually led the traveller to where it was buried and then disappeared. Liekkiös would also haunt buildings if their graves were beneath the floor. If a stranger stayed overnight, the liekkiö would try to contact him through dreams to show where it was buried.

Message: Liekkiö tells of opportunities left unused, of sorrow and loss. These losses may relate to relationships or forbidden feelings. Liekkiö is born from great injustice, from someone being denied life. Some part of you, an idea or an aspect of development, isn't getting the room it needs to emerge. The restricting energy may be coming from within yourself or from outside. Your community's attitudes may not support your own growth. Guilt may rear its head because of past mistakes that won't allow themselves to be forgotten. Face your buried memories and the energy linked to them will be released. Don't be too hard on yourself; it is through mistakes that you learn. If you have a worrying choice ahead, don't be afraid to choose the best option by listening to your heart.

FREEZING WIND
Four of Swords

FREEZING WIND

FOUR OF SWORDS

*Keywords: futile battle, defeat, wasting
energy, change of course.*

The freezing wind that sowed cold destruction and death was lovingly raised by Louhi, Mistress of Pohjola. Louhi kept the cold in the Stone-hill of Pohjola. After Lemminkäinen killed the

Master of Pohjola he fled to an island. The soldiers of Pohjola ransacked Lemminkäinen's mother's home while looking for him. Upon learning of the destruction when he returned, Lemminkäinen decided to retaliate. He asked Tiera, his brother-in-arms to go with him to Pohjola. Louhi sent a vicious frost against them, causing the sea to freeze over. Lemminkäinen made a fire, caught the cold with his bare hands and cast it into the flames. He sang a spell about the cold's birth, for any power could be controlled if its birth was known, and Lemminkäinen intended to destroy the cold. The cold began to beg for mercy. It proposed a truce, that neither would hurt the other. The truce was made and Lemminkäinen admitted defeat: Pohjola's power was too great for them to defy. It was a long, miserable journey over the ice back home for the two men.

MESSAGE: This card may refer to a conflict and power struggles may appear in relationships. If you are facing setbacks, as if you were walking against the wind, it may be appropriate to rethink whether you're going the right way. When you change your course the wind will be at your back and obstacles will vanish from your path. The human mind can sometimes make things hard by concentrating on worries and doubts. Don't give in; use your willpower to rise above doubt. Now is not a good time to fight. It's more fruitful to leave a conflicted situation behind and seek out an environment that supports your needs. Make a truce with the powers that oppose you instead of wasting your energy in an unnecessary power struggle.

FOLK OF THE GRAVEYARD
Five of Swords

FOLK OF THE GRAVEYARD

FIVE OF SWORDS

*Keywords: clinging onto the past, concern,
the need to correct things, forgiveness.*

The graveyard belonged to the dead. It was believed the first person to be buried to a graveyard would become its eternal keeper. Kalma was an invisible power associated with death.

It clutched to the boards a corpse had lain on, to its clothes and to the flowers placed on the grave. People tried to avoid it, for it could also cling to a human. Ghosts were restless dead who lingered between planes of existence harbouring personal tragedies. They couldn't release themselves from what had happened but mourned opportunities lost, yearned for justice, and couldn't forgive themselves or others. Ghosts could be so attached to a certain place, they wouldn't agree to leave it even after death. Most still living occupants found this extremely unpleasant and disturbing. If a person died because of violence or some other kind of trespass, a suicide or as a criminal, it was left to haunt the earth as a homeless soul.

MESSAGE: Spirits of the dead are ghosts of the past. Negative feelings aren't going anywhere, no matter how we might try to bury them. They will rise up again and again until we accept what has happened in our past. We must learn to forgive ourselves and others. Compassion towards one's own weaknesses enables compassion towards the weaknesses of others. The ghosts won't let you forget before the wrongs towards you and others have been made right. This card urges you to let go of the past and accept your own weaknesses. You are a lovable, brightly shining being despite your shadow. By facing your shadows, they may turn into new, invaluable assets. The fear we feel is a very powerful life-energy we may project towards constructive action. Dare to face unpleasant things directly and say what you know to be true.

ETIÄINEN
Six of Swords

ETIÄINEN

SIX OF SWORDS

*Keywords: premonitions, messages in
dreams, sudden changes, guidance.*

Etiäinen was part of every person's soul that appeared outside
of its master's body, received when a child was three days old.
It was an invisible doppelganger that sometimes walked before

its owner. Some people had it so strong that their etiäinen would arrive first. Occupants of the house would hear a horse and cart arrive and someone come to the door, but no one was to be seen. After some time, the etiäinen's master would arrive. Etiäinens were beyond their owner's control; they came and went as they pleased. They could appear to someone close to their owner as a sign of illness or death when their owner was on their deathbed. Etiäinen could also appear in a dream to tell about a coming event beforehand. The ancient Finns had many different beliefs regarding omens. Different kinds of signs could manifest as visions or premonitions. In Kalevala, the Mother of Lemminkäinen gets the news of her son's death at the River of Tuonela when a brush that he had struck at the wall started bleeding, just as he had said it would, should he perish.

MESSAGE: Etiäinen suggests that some kind of change is about to happen – stay vigilant and prepare for new things. Listen to what your intuition has to say. Etiäinen also brings news of unexpected choices you may not have considered before. Etiäinen is like a signpost that aids you in choosing the best of all available alternatives. Pay attention to your dreams and hunches. Have more trust in your instinct and listen what it has to say about your situation. Synchronisation is a sign from your guides that you're on the right path, appearing to those on their way to success. Door after door will open and new possibilities will appear when they are needed.

KAKKIAINEN
Seven of Swords

KAKKIAINEN

SEVEN OF SWORDS

*Keywords: misunderstandings, problems
that have built up, disturbance.*

Kakkiainens were tiny, obscure creatures, a kind of miniscule ghost.
Usually they lingered around churchyards and funeral processions.
Though not really dangerous, they were like tiny poltergeists that

delighted in causing difficulties and disturbances. Uncertainty made them go wild. It was important to clean one's house after visitors left, especially if there had been some quarrel. They flocked to where energy was unable to flow freely, where feelings were confined. Old grudges and arguments were their sustenance. Making a big deal out of problems and hanging on to small conflicts made the perfect environment for kakkiainens to run amok. When kakkiainens were around, even adults were prone to fits more befitting a toddler if they didn't get their way. Scrutinising other people's shortcomings and mistakes, condemning their beliefs and overall stalking were also kakkiainens' key characteristics.

MESSAGE: It is wise to take a constructive attitude towards the minor setbacks and conflicts you've faced. Don't overdramatise, be overly sensitive, nor harbour bitter thoughts, guilt or old grudges. It is better to just come out and say what is troubling you directly to the person involved; don't talk behind their back. The energy that travels between people forms a kind of link that binds them together on an energetic level. It is possible to sever these ties, and sometimes one simply must get rid of harmful relationships. Usually, though, it's enough when conflicts and hidden feelings are openly discussed. People judge others constantly and are mostly wrong because their motives come from their need to prop up their egos. Pay attention to your own condemning mind, for the mind is prone to divide everything into good and bad. Don't let the opinions of others bring you down – believe in yourself. Take care that you only associate with people who support your spiritual growth.

WITCHES' CIRCLE
Eight of Swords

WITCHES' CIRCLE

EIGHT OF SWORDS

*Keywords: freedom from mental shackles,
negative cycles, harbouring problems.*

A witches' circle was born when mushrooms grew to form a ring.
These circles were believed to have magical powers and were born
where fairies had danced. These circles weren't without danger,

for those who entered them might lose all sense of time, and the dance of the fairies might also escalate to such ferocity that a mere mortal could not endure it, but could lose their mind – or life. Fairies are often pictured as little girls and boys with wings, but originally they were small flying ghosts that looked like skinned squirrels and lingered around funeral processions and cemeteries. Where there were corpses, there were fairies. It was dangerous to associate with these creatures, for their power, which originated from death, might cling to humans and make them sick or even kill them. Fairies especially went after women who hadn't yet been cleansed by a priest's prayer after they had given birth. It was feared fairies would take the unbaptised child with them to their world.

Message: Witches' circle implies being imprisoned in a self-repeating pattern of events or thoughts. You may not realise how you build these situations yourself without learning anything from previous occasions. You may feel yourself a victim of circumstances, and these negative thoughts nourish the situation. Various addictions or obsessions may also be a sign of it. Old solutions just don't produce the desired outcome anymore. It's time to expand your circles, turn a critical eye towards the cycle your thoughts have created, and think in a new way. It's wise to check your own attitudes, instead of just grumbling and complaining. Only then will you be able to grow as a person and gain a new kind of aspect towards life that will break the cycle and release the energy trapped within.

WHITE DEER
Nine of Swords

WHITE DEER

NINE OF SWORDS

Keywords: trust, the right way, journey, enjoying life.

A white deer was a mythical creature capable of travelling between two worlds. It led to new paths and adventures, and new levels of consciousness. A symbol of purity, divinity and awakening, the white deer had a special stature, for white animals were thought to be sacred. To the Sami people, a white doe was a bringer of good luck believed to increase the herd's number, and they were sacrificed to gods associated with sky and wind. The hunt of a supernaturally fast elk or deer was a common legend throughout the world, as was the white deer. A well-meaning guide, it was also seen as a symbol of light, spirituality and nobility. The deer could be elusive and sometimes hunters were left chasing it for eternity. According to folklore, the line between human and animal was fickle, which is why skilled shamans and sages could assume the form of a deer when travelling the mountains of Lapland.

MESSAGE: The deer symbolises kindness, caring and gentleness, and is always vigilant to spot danger and flee. A fawn must learn to walk soon after it's born, so it may escape predators. This card refers to the detection of life's dangers and making quick decisions. It warns against sinking into a false sense of security so you won't be surprised. Deer also wander long distances and live freely, which could refer to a journey or a change of scenery. White deer refers to a spiritual journey during which the deer will act as a guide. The deer is connected to the ability to operate on two different levels, the physical and the spiritual. These levels are not contradictory towards each other, but support one another. You may make use of your spiritual capacity when faced with the boundaries of the physical world.

**COURT OF
SERPENTS**
Ten of Swords

COURT OF SERPENTS

TEN OF SWORDS

*Keywords: clarification, conversation,
resolving differences, facing the truth.*

A great white serpent carried the magical court-stone of serpents
in its mouth. The crown on its head emphasised its role as
king of snakes and keeper of wisdom. Other snakes sensed the

summons and gathered to hold court and find different aspects of truth. According to folklore, any object that had been in a serpent's mouth became a key that could open any lock. These kinds of objects could be used to heal the eyes through which we see the world. Serpents had a connection to both the afterlife and the renewing forces of life. They shed their skin, symbolising renewal and growth. Their forked tongue represented truth and lies. It was believed that one could learn to understand the language of birds by eating the flesh of a white snake. Birds never lied but spoke only the truth. Snakes were closely related to the underworld and Tuonela, to the powers below.

Message: The truth is not black and white; it has different sides and aspects. Try to listen to the perspectives of others with an open mind. It is said whoever tries to steal the court-stone will be hunted down by the snake-wheel, which symbolises the wheel of fate or karma. Honesty towards yourself and others is the only way to avoid being crushed by the snake-wheel. Honesty means having the courage to admit you are wrong if you have made a mistake. Only with a humble attitude is it possible for a person to assume the higher truth as his or her maxim. Are you ready to hear and tell the truth? Are you trying to hide your mistakes or do you admit it when you're wrong? To speak with the tongue of serpent is to speak with lies and deceit, for it has two forks, after all.

RAVEN
Page of Swords

RAVEN

PAGE OF SWORDS

Keywords: wisdom, intellectual clarity,
healthy selfishness, bargaining.

Ravens were believed to live for hundreds of years. In Finnish mythology, they were kept intelligent birds but often associated with dark forces and even death. According to folklore, black birds retrieved the souls of people who had done bad things when they died. That is why it was seen as a bad omen if black birds gathered in trees near houses. Witches were believed to take the form of a raven. The raven's nest was believed to contain a raven stone that made its owner invisible. According to folklore, one could learn the language of birds by eating a raven's egg. For hunters, ravens were lucky birds because they showed the whereabouts of prey. But raven was loyal to none but itself. In the *Kalevala,* the raven augurs the worse possible outcome to the Mother of Lemminkäinen when she's fishing the parts of her son's body from the black river of Tuonela. She nevertheless succeeds in reviving her son, despite the raven's opinion.

MESSAGE: Raven's power is in its mastery over its own life and the power to decide; it knows how to be selfish in a healthy manner. Raven teaches one to survive, think clearly and make choices for your own wellbeing. Raven is the harbinger of both light and dark, meaning it has an all-encompassing view of the situation. Nothing remains unseen from its eyes. It smells an opportunity before it arises, and whether it will be more trouble than it's worth. Raven is so perceptive it sees the future which makes it an excellent collaborator in challenging and changing situations of life. You must be ready to abandon old contracts and customs to keep up with the bird's quickly changing pace. It may change its mind at any moment and break old agreements when coming across new and better ones.

THE ELK OF HIISI
Knight of Swords

THE ELK OF HIISI

KNIGHT OF SWORDS

Keywords: grasping the challenge,
accomplishment, daring, problem-solving.

Lemminkäinen had arrived to propose to the Maid of Pohjola, and Louhi, her mother, ordered Lemminkäinen to first catch the Elk of Hiisi to prove himself. Lemminkäinen set after the animal, brimming with pride. He boasted there was no animal he couldn't take by surprise and carry home. Because of this bragging the folk of the woodland created a supernaturally fast elk that fled like the wind. Long did Lemminkäinen search the elk until he finally found its tracks in Lapland. He caught up to it and chased it into a corral. While stroking the animal's soft fur he fantasised how he would soon be making love to the Maid on the elk's soft pelt. But the elk heard these thoughts and grew enraged. It thrashed the corral and fled again. The crestfallen Lemminkäinen began to humbly chant spells and words of hunt. He travelled to the heart of the woodlands to meet Tapio, the god of the hunt, and his wife, Mielikki, and asked them to let him catch the elk. With his new, humble attitude he managed to find his quarry and to take it back to Pohjola to the ill-tempered Louhi.

MESSAGE: The Elk of Hiisi is about the passion of youth and about boldly taking on challenging tasks. Mere willingness won't be enough to attain your goal, it will also require discretion and control of thoughts. Problems can be solved through the wisdom brought by experience. Lemminkäinen thought the hunt for the elk would be an easy task and behaved arrogantly towards it. It was not until he halted and quit forcefully chasing his goals that he succeeded in earning the favour of gods, and was able to get what he was hoping for. The Elk of Hiisi represents the human mind, and control of thought is what this card is about.

ILMATAR
Queen of Swords

ILMATAR

QUEEN OF SWORDS

*Keywords: motherhood, taking on new
things, daring, compassion.*

Ilmatar, the maid of air who lived high above the clouds, grew
tired of her loneliness. 'What if I descended upon the foaming
waves?' she thought, and at once a gust of wind threw her down

to the sea. By sea and wind, she became pregnant and turned into Vellamo, the dame of water. Ilmatar carried her aching womb for years, praying to Ukko to release her from her torment. As she drifted on the waves, a diving duck searching the primordial sea for a place to nest flew past. It made its nest on the maid's knee, and as it laid its eggs, the knee began to heat. The maid shifted her leg and the eggs rolled into the sea and broke, and the world was born from their shards. As Ilmatar writhed in pain in the primordial sea, she inadvertently created the formation of the earth and water. Thirty years passed before Väinämöinen finally emerged from her womb. For eight years he drifted on the waves before washing up on a barren shore. Thus Väinämöinen was born from Ilmatar, who gave birth to the universe.

Message: Ilmatar represents feminine wisdom and deep vision. She doesn't hesitate to use her head but also doesn't forget the importance of heart. Ilmatar happened to shape the earth's formation almost accidentally while expecting Väinämöinen. It is often afterwards one notices how the hardships of the past have raised and shaped you, just like Ilmatar shaped the earth in her torment. Ilmatar left behind her heavenly home to give in to her destiny and something unique was born from her suffering. The greater the torments you face, the greater the things they are preparing you for. Bravely leave your comfort zone and dare to carry out your destiny. Trust in your own vision.

UKKO
King of Swords

UKKO

KING OF SWORDS

Keywords: all-encompassing vision, right kind of action, correct conclusions, sense of direction.

Ukko was the creator of thunder and light who struck the first spark of fire. Often seen as an old majestic lord, he rode his stone-cart across the skies during thunderstorms and threw his lightning bolts. It was believed that Ukko struck the clouds open with his lightning which allowed the invigorating rains to pour down on earth. Ukko was prayed to for rain for the crops, but also to prevent excessive downpours and storms. Demonic powers and all sorts of creatures were afraid of thunder and hid in their burrows. Ukko also provided cure for illnesses, and a sauna that was warmed by using wood from a tree that had been felled by lightning which had especially healing properties. People turned to him for help and his blessing, and when they were faced with labour or bleeding, hunting a bear or going to war. His protection was asked for grazing cattle as well as travellers.

MESSAGE: Ukko symbolises problem solving, intellect and authority without condemnation. He knows how to think flexibly, act quickly and make correct conclusions of a situation. He is a leader and has natural authority which he uses creatively in his actions, and he makes noble decisions. This kind of sublime state of mind is inside us all. This card urges you to grasp challenges and to have faith in yourself, and to use your intellect when making decisions. Thunder may also symbolise repressed feelings and warn you of bitterness and within you. Ukko's lightning bolts symbolises sudden inspiration and understanding. An inspiration or a new vision may strike suddenly. Lightning bolts also symbolises the force of life and illuminate the overcast sky. Clouds are thoughts and moods of the mind. You may suddenly figure out what something means or how something must be done to succeed.

FIELD PEKKO
Ace of Pentacles

FIELD PEKKO

ACE OF PENTACLES

Keywords: fertility, material and spiritual wellbeing, harvest.

Field Pekko watched over the growth of barley and protected the crop. The spirit lived in the field and could take the form of a white rabbit and show himself by running from one end of the field to the other. Pekko was worshipped and asked for help with the crop. People believed that Field Pekko aided in sowing during spring, made the land fertile and the ale – 'the milk of the field' – taste good. The first taste of every batch of ale was reserved for Pekko, and offered in the field where the barley had been harvested. In return he would make the crops grow, give the people a good mood and pick the bad grains away from the ears. Field Pekko could be made into a figure or a small statue that travelled from house to house every year. The statue was stored in the granary of the house, waiting for the sowing ceremonies the following spring.

MESSAGE: Field Pekko symbolises both inner and outer wealth developing in your life: luck, success, joy and bountiful times. The card urges committing oneself to a path on which spiritual and material wellbeing may flourish. It also offers the hope and promise of the harvest's abundance. The land is fertile and ready to take the seeds, symbolising the sowing of new ideas connected to the earth element. The time for harvest isn't necessarily current yet, but a developing process may demand patience and diligence from you. Take care of sowing your ideas in an accepting ground and actualising them in practice. A plentiful harvest will be your reward. Are you ready to receive luck and do everything you can for your own happiness? Give everything to the projects you feel inclined to and build your life to be ever happier and wealthier.

CAUGHT IN THE FOREST
Two of Pentacles

CAUGHT IN THE FOREST

TWO OF PENTACLES

*Keywords: breaking free from routine, communication
difficulties, need for own space, insecurity.*

While wandering in the woods, the folk of the earth could
begin to lead the traveller astray, which would put them under
a charm. Once caught in the forest, one could travel through

familiar places without recognising them or walk in circles indefinitely. The forest could also cover the person or animal completely from human eyes and disguise them as fallen logs, stones or tree stumps. A person caught in the forest could see and hear everything that happened around them but couldn't move or speak. Children caught in the forest would say they hadn't been hungry, for birds and frogs had brought them berries and other edibles. To be freed from this charm, one could turn one's clothes inside out and change shoes to the wrong feet. If one was able to move, it was wise to head back the opposite way one came, which would suddenly lead home. Another way to be freed was to bind the forest, by bending a branch into a loop with the help of a stone, and then releasing it.

MESSAGE: This card may be a sign of the need to retreat from the maelstrom of life and seek some peace and quiet. Being alone may help you unify your energies and gather your thoughts. Silence is the state from whence new thoughts and perspectives may be born. In relationships, the card can mean the need for your own space. The person caught in the forest was unable to express themselves. Instead of withdrawing, the card urges you to talk and face problems. This card may also symbolise getting inadvertently lost. It is time to stop and think about your life, relationships, choices and path. The folklore's advice to turn ones clothes inside out to be freed could be seen as reversing one's attitudes and roles.

TONTTU
Three of Pentacles

TONTTU

THREE OF PENTACLES

*Keywords: diligence, self-control, sense
of duty, fortunate life-changes.*

Tonttu was a house elf who took care of the happiness and
order of the house. The name is derived from the Finnish
word *tontti*, the spirits of certain places. One could find several

tonttus around the homestead: Saunatonttu lived in the sauna, Milltonttu in the mill, Stabletonttu in the stable and so forth. Food was provided for the elves to keep them favourable. Some tonttus had a ghostlike appearance and could look like the household's head. Some were like small ancient men covered in mould, and some had one great eye in the middle of their forehead. Tonttus usually stayed invisible, but one could still hear them go bump in the night. If a tonttu showed itself, it was thought to be an omen of some coming misfortune, but the tonttu's intention was only to help. Sometimes they woke residents at night to warn of fire or an animal in distress. Tonttus didn't suffer quarrelsome or raucous behaviour. An angered tonttu might leave, and the house would become impoverished.

MESSAGE: Tonttu is a diligent labourer with a strong sense of duty. This card symbolises discipline and plans being actualised. As a counterbalance to work, a peaceful home supports your endeavours. Now is a good time to leap into action, and finish off incomplete projects. Tonttu may also refer to the ability to enjoy your work. The card may foretell of changes in the family – moving house, a birth, marriage, new job or profession. Tonttu predicts stability, continuity and coming wealth. Tonttus would fight with each other if certain boundaries weren't respected. This may symbolise competing projects hindering each other's completion. Try to prioritise the projects most important to you and finish them first. Tonttu may also mean running the risk of overachieving leading to burn out, so take care not to overdo it.

KRATTI
Four of Pentacles

KRATTI

FOUR OF PENTACLES

Keywords: wealth, property, preservation,
financial discretion.

Krattis were elves whose mission was to guard buried treasure.
Described as brown, furry creatures or a small old man with
a beard green with mould, they didn't spend a single coin from

the treasure. Krattis never left their treasure. During the night of the Midsummer day, they would lift the treasure above ground and burn a treasure-flame on it, to burn the mould and dirt away. Old tales say that bracken blooms only at night, and if one took a blooming bracken to the fire, the treasure would be theirs. The treasure seeker had to be a brave soul though, for all sorts of abominations lingered there, and they had to be passed without fear. A black animal could be sacrificed when the treasure was buried, thus making the sacrificed creature its guardian. The treasure could only be found by making the same kind of sacrifice. In the grimmest tales, the sacrifices were little children. It was possible to find the treasure by simply digging where the trove was known to be, but this was dangerous – the kratti in no circumstances was going to forfeit its treasure to anyone.

MESSAGE: Kratti's life purpose is to guard the treasure. Kratti symbolises a person who has mettle and patience. The card urges you to take care of your finances and property, and your personal limits. Kratti prefers to be in control instead of sharing its responsibilities and wealth with others. This may be a sign of independence or selfishness, depending on the situation. Kratti advises you to consider all proposals carefully and to scrutinise the fine print. This card may also symbolise setting limits or hiding behind excessive walls. In human relationships, the card can mean setting boundaries, but also being afraid to open one's heart and reveal one's true feelings and thoughts to another.

MILK PARA
Five of Pentacles

MILK PARA

FIVE OF PENTACLES

Keywords: comparison, worry, pessimism,
spiritual and material independence.

Milk paras were supernatural beings who stole cream from the neighbours' containers or sucked milk straight from their cows. It carried what it had stolen in its flagon-like stomach to its master, and regurgitated the milk or cream into a churn. When a para's sharp teeth left wounds on the cows' udders causing mastitis, it was a sign a para had made a visit. A para was created by using rags, bones, wool and animal fur, sometimes even human bones, usually by the mistress of the house, who would also add drops of blood from her own finger. Its legs were made from spindles or knitting needles, and it was brought to life during magical moments such as Christmas or Midsummer by spells and incantations in a sauna, mimicking a real birth. A yellow slime mould, *Fuligo septica*, that sometimes appeared around houses or pastures was called 'para's faeces', and it could be used to identify a para's owner. One simply had to whip the mould, which would force the guilty mistress to appear. The mould's appearance could very well be deemed sufficient evidence in a witch trial.

MESSAGE: This card is often a sign your attention is focused on what you don't have, instead of being grateful for what you do. It is senseless to compare yourself and your life to those of others. Focus on your own life and work towards getting your affairs in order. This card means that something is gnawing at your happiness. Milk para urges you to inspect the movements of your own mind. This card may also signify victim mentality or martyrdom. Such thoughts prevent you from seeing the cause and effect relations of things. Milk para urges you to look in the mirror and realise how you yourself have affected the situations and happenings in your life.

DOMESTIC SNAKES
Six of Pentacles

DOMESTIC SNAKES

SIX OF PENTACLES

*Keywords: generosity, compassion,
fertility, increase of wealth.*

Domestic snakes were harmless grass snakes that lived around
the courtyard, in the cow-shed, under the residence, in the
sauna or under stone-piles that were sometimes built for them

150

beneath sacrificial trees. Their purpose was to protect the cattle, bring wealth and help people to conceive. Some houses only had one snake, but there are tales of cow-sheds teeming with them. Killing a domestic snake would bring misfortune, such as the death of the house's best cow. The first milk and grain of the season were sacrificed to the snakes. Some women even gave their first breast milk to them to show their gratitude for giving her a child. Dead snakes or parts of them might also be hidden in the structures when a new house was built, to protect it.

MESSAGE: Domestic snakes relates to a happy family life and an increase of wellbeing in the home. The card also represents sexuality, passion, fertility and wealth since snakes protected cattle. Snakes are very different to humans and fear is a natural reaction to everything different. That is why the card urges you to be tolerant and to understand and accept different things. The card also relates to compassion and generosity. The snakes were not disturbed, so they did not harm people either. Tolerance of diversity and kindness towards others is the central theme of the card. This card may also suggest exploitation and living off others. In this case the benefactor is feeding the snakes because of fear of what might happen if they stop, and their actions aren't altruistic anymore. Domestic snakes may warn you of people who would gladly pick the cherries off the cake but not help in baking it. It may be a call for you to awaken to realise what has slithered into your life.

MOUNTAIN TROLLS
Seven of Pentacles

MOUNTAIN TROLLS

SEVEN OF PENTACLES

Keywords: hardships, to go astray,
mixed feelings, determination.

Trolls were sharp-toothed, hairy, beastlike creatures that lived inside mountains and great rocks. They were simple creatures and could be troublesome neighbours. They loved to ransack houses and let cows loose from the shed. Trolls could come a-knocking and ask to borrow something, but they always used strange names for the things they wanted and never returned them. Trolls loved music and were seen dancing around great bonfires. Their leader, Big Murk, was larger than the others and only had one eye. Some trolls delighted in inviting humans into their caves and getting them lost underground. These kinds of invitations were best turned down, as trolls had nothing more than snot and garbage to offer their guests. Sometimes trolls gave gifts – at night the present could look like a bagful of shavings, but in the morning it could prove to be pure gold.

MESSAGE: Mountain trolls may suggest misunderstandings and conflicts in life. Trolls don't call things by their proper names, which can easily lead to misunderstanding and trouble. The card can reflect irresponsible behaviour, selfishness, blaming others, provocation and swelling of problems. Try to maintain your self-control even in difficult situations and remain objective. Also try to understand your opponent's motivations; constructive solutions can be found through cooperation. Trolls may be violent and impetuous, and the card's challenges may relate to dealing with this sort of person. Mountains symbolise perspective, clarity, spiritual consciousness and strength, and these qualities are what is needed when dealing with trolls. Firmly say no; set clear boundaries, for they won't give mercy if they get the upper hand. Troll-gold can be seen as a metaphor for challenges that at first seem to bring with them only bad experiences, but which later turn out to be valuable life lessons.

MAAHINEN
Eight of Pentacles

MAAHINEN

EIGHT OF PENTACLES

*Keywords: enjoyment of work, life
management, routines, physical actions.*

Maahinens were folk who lived underground, in a world where
everything was opposite to ours. They walked with their feet
towards the sky, left and right were contrariwise and so were

night and day; even trees grew upside-down. Those who lived there were sometimes thought to be spirits of the dead, who continued their life down below with their families. Maahinens were small, brownish creatures who could change their form; they often visited the world above as ants or frogs. It was unwise to step on the path of ants for it might very well be a path of maahinens, and they could make the person get lost in the forest. Maahinens lived like humans, raising cattle and practising agriculture and crafts. They married, had children and grew old just like humans. Maahinens didn't really care for their elderly and tried from time to time to change them for human children. Unbaptised children were especially in danger of being swapped.

Message: Maahinen represents hard work, enjoyment of work, smooth everyday routines, order, efficiency and conscientiousness. When a person has a strong connection to the energies of the earth, they are healthy, balanced and successful. If the connection to these energies is absent or weak, a person is unable to grasp daily chores. This weak connection is easy to notice in small setbacks: stubbing your toe, forgetting your keys, missing the bus, forgetting what you had to buy from the store. If this happens all the time, it is time to ground yourself. Sit comfortably, breathe calmly and close your eyes. The earth's energy is dark – picture it rising along your spine while you 'grow' yourself roots deep into the earth. Unnecessary troubles disappear with a calm walk in the woods. Maahinen urges you to live in harmony with your environment.

STONE LABYRINTH
Nine of Pentacles

STONE LABYRINTH

NINE OF PENTACLES

*Keywords: fulfilment, spiritual reserves,
conquering great challenges.*

The giants of Finnish folklore possessed supernatural strength,
flinging gigantic boulders to peculiar places when angered.
Sometimes they carried them in their pockets, from where they

fell. Such rocks were called purse-stones. In some tales the giants also helped humans by carrying stones from which churches or bridges were built, or by bringing huge amounts of gravel to where a new road was built. Ancient labyrinths made of stones are known as giant's gardens and are suspected to have been ritualistic places. The ones near coasts may be the work of fishermen or sailors, who made them just to pass the time or to pray to higher powers for large catches or favourable winds. Giant's gardens may also have been used to mark borders, seeing as they are usually located in remote places and on islands. If the stones of the labyrinth were moved, they always returned to their places by themselves. You were not allowed to take stones with you or a punishment followed and the nature spirits would not leave you alone.

MESSAGE: Stone labyrinth means a closing circle, something becoming complete. You are bringing things to an end and your reserves will be restored and a deep calm will fill your mind. You have every reason to be proud of your accomplishments. No challenge is too great not to be conquered with the help of one's own inner strength. You are strong both spiritually and physically. Now is a good time to finish all incomplete projects. The stone labyrinth is a symbol of perfection and harmony. Every stone is in its place forming a harmonious entirety reflecting the peace of mind and things finding their proper place. You will notice if something isn't in harmony in your life. When plagued by fears or doubts concentrate on thinking that everything will work out.

PIRITYINEN
Ten of Pentacles

PIRITYINEN

TEN OF PENTACLES

*Keywords: luck with money,
immortality, rebirth, blessings.*

A pirityinen was a small creature that looked like a bee or
dorbeetle believed to bring money, luck and success to its
owner. It was said that a person who owned a pirityinen would

never run out of money. Also known as the 'money-devil', the creature was kept in an upholstered bottle or tin-box, and its owner would feed it their own spit and blood. A pirityinen was strongly attached to its owner on a spiritual level and kept on bringing riches no matter what. It would follow its owner to their deathbed, and after the owner had passed on, crawl into their mouth. It was customary to place a coin into the dead person's mouth as payment to get them across the River of Tuonela, and perhaps the pirityinen knew this and crawled into its owner's mouth to get to the afterlife with them.

MESSAGE: Pirityinen is a message that a richer life is about to begin. You've worked hard and payday has arrived. Your financial matters may suddenly begin to go more smoothly; perhaps you may get a new job or a raise, or win the lottery. This card says it's time to enjoy the abundance and riches you will receive. Yet it also says you mustn't be jealous or bellyache about your lot, or you will get nothing. The more thankful we are, the more we shall receive. Pirityinen challenges your relationship towards fortune and money. Do you have enough or are you hoarding? Do you know how to share your wealth with others? Pirityinen may also manifest in the form of some other precious, immaterial thing. The dorbeetle represents creation, immortality and rebirth, and protects its owner from all evil, but pirityinen reminds us spiritual wealth is the only thing we can take to the other side.

FOREST MAIDEN
Page of Pentacles

FOREST MAIDEN

PAGE OF PENTACLES

Keywords: fortunate coincidence,
interaction, spontaneity, adventure.

The maidens who watched over the forests were benevolent, guiding those who had lost their way and warned of dangers. A forest maiden would wake a person spending their night in the forest if their fire was about to spread, a snake was about to slither into their trouser leg, or some predator was drawing near. It was best to greet them when entering the forest as they liked a polite approach. As a reward the maidens could guide a traveller to mushrooms or berries, or shoo animals to the hunter's path. If one had trouble getting a fire going in the forest, it might've been because it was on the forest maiden's path. When willing, forest maidens could change their height to that of a tall tree or a blade of grass. Forest maidens would appear at the fire to warm themselves, acting all come-hither, but come dawn they would be gone or disguised as moss, rocks or tree stumps.

MESSAGE: Forest maiden's message is to have an unprejudiced attitude when you are having new experiences, and to have a playful attitude towards life. A fortunate coincidence may bring great joy into your life. Forest maiden urges you to use your imagination and not to rationalise things too much. The card reminds you that the things you wish would come into your life already exist, even though you may not have caught them yet. One day they will arrive, real and tangible. Forest maiden urges you to live in the present moment, but at the same time to dream of something better. When the maiden wakens the one sleeping in the forest, it means that something is driving you away from an unfavourable situation. Heed the call you hear in your heart. Tread your own path.

BEAR
Knight of Pentacles

BEAR

KNIGHT OF PENTACLES

Keywords: yearly cycle, strength, patience, right timing.

Bear was born in heaven at the bosom of Otava, the constellation known as Ursa Major, from whence it was lowered to earth with silver chains in a golden basket. According to fable, the bear and a human woman once had a relationship, and the bearfolk of the Forest Finns were born from this union. The Finnish and Karelian languages have over two hundred words for bear – a sign of deep reverence towards this king of the forest. Only men were allowed to hunt the bear; women were not even allowed to touch the hunting spears or eat the animal's meat so that the hunting luck wouldn't be spoiled. A sleeping bear was out of bounds; it had to be awakened before it was attacked, especially if it was hibernating. The bear was precious quarry, and a great feast was always prepared after one was killed. A symbolic wedding was held to unite the bear with its bride, and the feast could go on for days.

MESSAGE: Bear is about amassing strength and becoming whole, but remaining sensitive. It refers to the spontaneous creativity that comes from the pure joy of expressing oneself. You are following your own path, and the opinions of others hold no sway over you. You have a thick skin just like a bear. Your self-confidence is deep and past experiences have made you strong. Bear's habit of hibernating refers to patience and also drawing wisdom from the dream-world. Bear also refers to the cycle of life. It may mean that some era in your life is about to begin or end. This card tells of deep reverence towards life's fundamental values, of appreciation of comforts, and of adaptability. Bear is a good card when associated to undertakings that require stamina and patience. It is a master of right timing.

MIELIKKI
Queen of Pentacles

MIELIKKI

QUEEN OF PENTACLES

*Keywords: lifeforce, mental and
physical wellbeing, continuity.*

Mielikki was the mistress of forests governing over the vast
granaries of Tapiola. All quarry was called grain of the forest,
and Mielikki had the golden keys that opened the granaries.

She took care of the forest's beauty, balance and harmony, and the wellbeing of the plants. She knew the healing properties of plants and how to use them, and every *emuu* (derived from *emo*, meaning 'mother') accompanied her. Each plant and animal had its own emuu, a progenitor that had given birth to its kind. The emuu was the one who decided to whom it gave one of its children as quarry. The emuu was contacted and appeased beforehand, so it would give one of its offspring for quarry. If the emuu complied and the hunt was successful, the hunters would throw a great feast. Their purpose was to return the dead animal's soul to the spirit-world through various rites and thank the animal for sacrificing itself. The quarries could also be revered by burying their bones in their proper order. Mielikki was thanked with gifts when a hunt was successful.

MESSAGE: Mielikki is benevolent and filled with feminine care and love. The mistress of forests appreciates and respects every living thing, taking care of the environment and protecting all life. She also knows how to take care of herself. Mielikki reminds you that you deserve all bounty that comes to you. Selfishness, pride and laziness may cause Mielikki to lock her granaries. This happened to Lemminkäinen when he was on the trail of the Elk of Hiisi. He was egocentric and proud, which didn't amuse the mistress of forests, and she wouldn't soften before Lemminkäinen humbled himself. Remember you won't always get what you want, but what you need. Mielikki also symbolises mother earth, giver of life, fertility, creativity and strength.

TAPIO
King of Pentacles

TAPIO

KING OF PENTACLES

*Keywords: ability to enjoy life, gentle
leadership, practicality, reliability.*

Tapio was the lord of the woodlands and sometimes appeared
as a mossy-bearded man as tall as the tallest spruces; even today
his face can be discerned tree trunks, if you know where to look.

Tapio planted every tree and plant in the forest, and elk and deer were his to give as quarry. Tapio had to be respected, or one could find themselves face to face with the forest lord's dark side. When Tapio was in a good mood, luck would be on a hunter's side; but for those who defiled the forest by trampling anthills or killing endangered animals, Tapio would manifest as anger incarnate. These intruders had no hope of catching anything and would suffer accidents such as snakebites. 'So the forest answers as one shouts' as the old Finnish proverb goes. A part of the first kill was sacrificed to Tapio in a sacred place in the forest known as Tapio's tables.

MESSAGE: Tapio is a just, gentle leader who knows how to keep his dignity. This card refers to practicality, industry, spiritual and physical bounty, and wellbeing. It also refers to a person who enjoys life and strives to provide a secure foundation for their loved ones. This card urges you to respect what you do for a living. Ideally, every person would be employed in work they are good at and enjoy. How can you find more pleasure in your job? If you find no joy at all, is there something you could do instead? The forest symbolises the subconscious and the different paths that lead there, so check your attitude. The forest has been a sacred place to the Finns, a place to quieten and calm. This card may also mean trying to see the forest from the trees, and discerning important things from less important.

About the author

Susanna Elina Salo was born and raised in Helsinki, the capital of Finland. In her work, she brings Finnish and Karelian old mythology and folklore into a form that is easily accessible. Influenced by folklore and mythological creatures, the wisdom of her cards springs from her Finnish roots. Susanna's goal is to always find something behind the myth that anyone can relate to in their own life, so brings the characters, events and creatures of mythology into modern times.

A self-taught artist and painter, Susanna illustrated most of the cards herself. She loves learning new painting techniques and trying out new ideas. As an illustrator, she wants to give visual form to mythological creatures, characters and events. In her free time, Susanna likes to be in nature, explore the old holy places of Finnish nature, pick mushrooms and berries and take care of her vegetable garden. Susanna loves growing different herbs and vegetables and gardening is her way to relax. A committed forager, she often cooks with nature's bounty. Susanna also has a passion for medicinal herbs.

🔘 ukonpakkatarot
🔘 mythologiafennicatarot